BORN

BORN

Giving Birth to a New You

By Dee Wallace

810 Eastgate North Drive, Suite 200
Cincinnati, OH 45245

ISBN: 978-1-956216-02-8

Briton Publishing, LLC Books are distributed by Ingram Content Group.

Books by Dee Wallace

BuppaLaPaloo

Conscious Creation

The Big E!

Bright Light

Getting Stuff

Wake Up Now!

Table of Contents

PREFACE

I've wanted to write this book for years now. After working with thousands of clients to release their limiting beliefs, empower themselves, and create the lives they want, I realized how the truth of religion, the core of spirituality, and the facts of brain science were all saying the same thing: It's all about Love.

I know, at the onset, Love doesn't necessarily harmonize with the concepts of brain science, until you understand how energy works. And that is what this book will explain in really simple terms that everyone can understand: how energy works and how you can direct it with a simple formula that allows you to create everything you want in life.

When my channel first opened up, I questioned why I was chosen to bring in this information. Do you want to hear the answer? Because I was "the girl next door." I was naïve enough to believe this message; I spoke simply and directly, bolstered by an English and Theatre Degree; and I loved to teach. My biggest issue was self-trust. After all these years, I can say unequivocally that I have never known my channel to be wrong.

When I was young, I had several experiences of connecting with the information "out there." I would hear voices with messages, receive guidance, even interacted with energy (my father) after his suicide. Now, to be clear, all children have such experiences, or to some extent. Ever hear of an imaginary friend? Fortunately, my mother didn't shame me or laugh at me when I told her my musings. One night, when I was around eight years old, I woke her up to say that something was wrong at grandma's house. Bless her, she got up and called. No answer. Bless her, we drove over to her home at three a.m. The cat had climbed up on the stove and turned all the burners on filling the air with gas. Grandma was okay but groggy. Who knows how she would have fared by morning? I always appreciated how my mother respected me enough to listen to my "musings" and believed in me. Looking back, that was the start of giving myself permission to trust the information I received.

I actually "spoke" to my father after his suicide through a light that entered my bedroom. He told me it "wasn't my fault" and that I should go on and be happy. It was a weird experience because I wasn't afraid at all. It wasn't spooky, but peaceful. And I felt a lot of love from him. That doesn't happen if you are scared that it's a bogeyman!

I share these impressions from my childhood to show why moving into channeling seemed so natural to me. I just trusted the experiences. Then, later in life, as I made my way as an actress, I found a mentor, Charles Conrad, who taught us how to tap into energy and "channel" the character! Of course, he didn't call it that, but when I began channeling, I realized that I had been doing this for years in my acting. Channeling bestows freedom on you; freedom from doubting and pondering and struggling. All thoughts and possibilities are open to all of us. But, as the Good Book says, you must ask to receive. You have to state: "I want the highest information and guidance about this subject now. I want to know." And doubt will never bring that to you. But we will delve with more depth into this conduit in the book.

This work and these teachings have changed my life. For thousands of my clients, some of whose stories are included here, it has also changed their lives. Keep an open mind. Be open to all the possibilities of You! On this plane, you literally ARE your own creator through your thoughts, feelings, and beliefs. This book will help you embrace your creative power with zest and fun and commitment. You will understand how it all works, and how to apply it. Most importantly, you'll know it is not just luck or happenstance. It is real, and you can do it!

EARLY PRAISES

"You'll have a smile on your face from the first page of this book. Dee Wallace covers the universal principles of creation and manifestation in a way that crackles with life and humor. Simple, practical exercises focus your intentions and align them with your highest good. Dee has worked with thousands of clients, and illustrates her practical teachings with inspiring stories of how they succeeded. You'll see how it often takes just a tiny shift in thought and feeling to make dramatic changes to your external circumstances. While enjoying Dee's bright, lively energy, laced with fun and intuitive examples, you'll find this short primer to be direct, warm and actionable." — Dawson Church, best-selling author of *Bliss Brain: The Neuroscience of Remodeling Your Brain for Resilience, Creativity and Joy*

* * * * *

"This book is a 'must read' for anyone interested in co-creating a life that is aligned with their highest potential. Even if you think your life is perfect, there is still something here for you. Dee beautifully explains how you can release limiting beliefs and create the life you want. She gives us wonderful examples from her own experiences and provides ample tools and exercises for the reader to truly become a master of their own destiny." — Lee Carroll, *Channel for KRYON*

* * * * *

"I have read everything in the manifestation genre, but Dee Wallace's *Born*, is my new Bible." — John Nelson, author of *A Guide to Energetic Healing*

* * * * *

"Dee uses an amazing and unique amalgamation of science, spirituality, energy healing and even religious text to reveal the truest steps, the purest mindsets, and the most comprehensive understandings, to create anything you want in your life. If you are ready to take command and guide your life adventure to whole new levels of manifestation, ease, grace (and EVEN happiness), then pick up this book and don't put it down until you've read it a bunch of times. Warning, your life is about to change in every way for the better, so get ready." — Jennifer McLean, *Celebrated Energy Medicine Healer, Creator of The Spontaneous Transformation Technique*

* * * * *

"Born is one of those rare books that provides the simplicity of truth, combining the backing of science and Dee's and her clients' spiritual journeys, and changes the way you think and feel about yourself. I experienced so many epiphanies by the first three chapters that I finally had to pause and grab my highlighter so that I could easily reference the multitudes of 'aha' moments I was experiencing." — John Burgos, Spiritual Activist and Host, *Beyond the Ordinary Show*

"This work has changed my life. It has allowed me to manifest things beyond my wildest dreams—and this book is the only thing you need to learn how to do it all." — Gabrielle Stone, two-time best-selling author

* * * * *

"Like E.T.'s famous phone call home, Dee Wallace's, *Born,* is an invitation for you to call the Universe in order to manifest all the love, health and prosperity that you desire. Filled with fascinating personal anecdotes, stories, and science, these pages offer a clear and concise roadmap for using intentionality, energy and love in ways that align you with unlimited possibility and creativity. Don't wait another moment to get started on this journey to shine your light of joy and love into the world! Dee Wallace's, *Born* is a masterful and inspired love letter written to the self-creating Universe—and that means you." — Donald Altman, best-selling author of *The Mindfulness Toolbox, Simply Mindful,* and the novel *Travelers*

CHAPTER ONE: ENERGY

Everything is energy. And that's all there is to it.

Albert Einstein

Everything is energy: me, you, the tree, a thought, a feeling, a belief, a flower. When anything dies, the energy of its being flows back into the reservoir of all energy until it returns to the material plane under the direction of . . . something or someone. And therein lies the secret. Energy must be directed. Aristotle put it this way: "The energy of the mind is the essence of life." Oprah has said: "You are responsible for the energy that you create for yourself. Great minds think alike!"

But before we delve into specifics, let's review some fundamental truths: 1) everything is energy, 2) energy has always been and always will be, 3) energy carries consciousness through frequency modulation (if you are angry, you express the frequency of anger, and if joyful, the frequency of joy) and 4) energy is an electromagnetic force that creates through intention and direction (your thoughts from your mind and the feelings from your heart are electrical messages to the Universe.)

We are both the creative force that chooses and directs energy, AND the creative force that demands energy to follow our clear intention. Thus, we are, literally, the formative element of creation Itself. It is a true statement that no one can think a thought for you. Correct? And no one can feel a feeling for you. Correct? And no one can hold a belief for you. Correct? That means you are in control of choosing the thoughts, feelings and beliefs that create your reality, and the energy of you must be directed through choice by . . . you.

Let's say you want to make ice. You know that because you have a thought to make ice, which translates into an intention. So, you physically direct yourself (the energy of you) to take creative action: get the ice tray, pour the water into it, and place the tray in the freezer. You and your freezer work together, from your intention, to make ice! You and the Universe work together in the same way in the creation of your life. You have a wish, dream, or a need that creates your intention, and you want to take action to create it. But before you can manifest it, you must do the inner work to bring the creative force into harmony with your intention. You made ice because you knew you would feel better with that ice in a nice cold drink. You "felt" that pleasure, and creation was easy! And the same applies to money, success, great relationships, health etc.

18

But most of us are not using our energy in partnership with the Universe from that feeling good, all-knowing place.

For example, you could not make ice if you put mud into the tray. Mud does not resonate with "ice," or your feelings about its benefits. Using the same principle, you cannot create money by resenting it, which counters your intention. The two "elements" don't "resonate." So the Universe, the delivery system, cannot create the desired results. Know that the Universe has no agenda here. It has no "intention" other than continually aligning the frequencies of your intent with your actions. Good/bad. Positive/negative. The Universe doesn't judge. It only matches up to your signals and delivers.

The easiest way to align intention with pure action is to be in a state of love. This state rejects actions counter to our best intentions, because we choose to do only what resonates with the state of love. Living in fear, anger, and worry is like trying to make ice from mud. Dwelling on our old stories of victimhood cannot create the electrical frequency of love that the Universe can match. In the state of love, we are not judging. We are not in fear. When we are in the state of love, we are at that zero point where we can choose to focus on the positive creations that we want, instead of allowing our monkey-mind with its doubts to "muddy" the signals. So being in the state of love is imperative for creating what we want. Ask yourself: Do you love everything you want to create, or are you in judgment or resentment toward

19

it? Are you in harmony with the partner you want, or are you focused on the jerks or dingbats of your tattered history, those you don't want again? No harmony! Do you love your body, or are you judging it for "not being right?" No harmony! We'll take a much closer look at this in Chapter 3. Right now, let's keep focused on Energy.

Here are the principles of energy:

1) That's all there is. When you break down the structure of an atom (the basic building block of matter), all you find is energy.

2) It is available to everyone equally.

3) Energy must be directed consciously, or it will get directed by anything or anyone that draws its attention. For example, television commercials can subliminally direct your energy to create sickness by associating a minor discomfort with a major illness, and one requiring their pills to cure, while showing you pictures of happy families and dogs. If you are unconscious, your mind gets the message that, "sickness and happiness go together." Energy also can be directed by old fears and beliefs you have been taught or experienced. When you become conscious that those beliefs are running you,

then you take back your power and direct your energy toward what you really desire.

4) Energy is the Creative Force of the Universe. It's like the flour in bread. It is an integral part of making the bread, but what you do with it, or how you put it together with the other components of the recipe, creates the outcome—a good loaf of bread, or not. Or, in another context, a successful life of conscious creation. Or not.

5) When energy is in alignment and harmony with love and joy, the masculine and feminine aspects become balanced. Your heart opens, your chakras open, and you stay in your Knowing, instead of diving into doubt. You trust yourself to create your best self. This becomes easier the longer you practice conscious creation, because you get proof from your manifestation.

6) When energy is in alignment and harmony with love and joy, you know you are complete. Remember, love and joy are choices!

We'll delve into these concepts with greater detail later in the book, and you will absolutely know how to live the principles taught here to create the life you want. But you must know and accept the activation principles laid out here because they are the keys to building everything else. I want to be clear that what I write about here embraces the core beliefs of all religions and faiths, as you will see. The principles of truth are constant. They have been presented in different creeds down through the ages, but the truth of these concepts is the same.

I would like to propose that, for this discussion, we use "all thought and all possibility" and "Creative Force" as our all-encompassing terms for God, Buddha, Energy, Krishna, etc. After all, does not the very definition of these entities as omnipresent and omniscient imply as much? This formulation will allow us to detach from any negative or fearful messages and beliefs taught to us. These may include: we have no power, and it's all up to God; we don't deserve to get what we want; we are sinners who have to pay for our transgressions; it's all up to fate, etc. Such belief systems have limited us for lifetimes. But they are false representations of the core truths of all Truth. Because you see, creative energy is neutral. It does not judge. It only matches frequencies. So, ultimately, we must access and BE the frequency of what we want. BE the frequency of all thought and all possibilities, which resonates with love and joy. So, as stated earlier, let's call the all-encompassing activating principle: Creative Force.

The challenge for us is that we have free choice. This means we must choose what we want and choose the thoughts, feelings, beliefs and actions that deliver it, like making ice! Or accumulating money. Or attracting a divine partner. Or being successful.

So, out of all the thoughts and possibilities out there, we must choose what we want by what we think about it, how we feel about it, and what we focus on. Or, our unconscious history of negative attitudes and experiences will choose it for us. We must step forward to take responsibility for our self-creation because energy must and will follow direction. Now, all the above great teachers have one pivotal principle in common: LOVE. Scientists are now in agreement that the power of love affects us even at a cellular level. So, let's come together in this exploration and agree that:

1) We have dominion over our thoughts and feelings, and beliefs, which are made up of energy.

2) Energy follows directions.

3) We are responsible for choosing how we direct our energy.

4) Energy does not question, judge, give, or deny. It simply follows the direction it receives through our thoughts and feelings and belief systems.

5) It is in direct dialogue with the Creative Force (all thought and possibility).

6) Love is the greatest Creative Force on Earth. It encompasses all other higher forms of creation. Bottom line: if you do not love yourself, you will not choose to give yourself what you desire.

We now have a great platform to build on. I really want you to understand these principles. Ever hear the saying, "God helps him who helps himself"? This maxim is how embodiment works. We have been given the power ("you are made in the image and likeness of me") to choose from all the positive possibilities of creation ("these miracles and more will you do also.") But, on this plane, we must learn how to work with energy, through love, and direct it toward what we want. We are here to learn and master creation through the use of energy to honor ourselves and all creators.

It says very clearly in the *I Am Discourses* of Saint Germain, that The Creative Force cannot, and will not, intercede on our behalf without our "clear direction." But we have been taught to wait. To wait for what we want to be given to us. And most of the time, while waiting, we still believe that we are not worthy to receive the very thing we hope to attract! I would be confounded if I were the Creative Force! So . . . you want it, but

I shouldn't give it to you because you don't deserve it? Okay, the Universe says, I will just . . . wait . . . until you get clear about what you are asking for, and until you know you deserve it! Don't wait! Create!

And I want to address that crucial word "ask." We all know the Biblical passage, "Ask and it shall be given to you." (Matthew 7:7) But do you know that in the Hebrew language, in which the Bible was written, "ask" means "claim or demand"? So, it's more of a power statement, "This will be delivered to me now." Energetically, that makes a big difference in how the Universe lines up and delivers on your request. We'll delve into the exact specifics of how this little dance works in Chapter 3.

When we can finally accept that we are the power, the love, the joy, and the choice that creates our lives, then all the energy of the Universe can partner with us: that's 200 billion galaxies and counting! We have now defined ourselves as self-creators who, working with the Creative Force, can create and manifest anything. But, until we accept and commit to this principle, we are waiting. And we know how energy responds to waiting. It . . . waits. And not much moves forward. If we live in the "I don't know what I want," place, we usually stop trying to create because, literally, we are stopping or sabotaging ourselves from even starting. Bottom line, if you know what you don't want (the negative), then you know what you DO want (the positive.) Then you can ask/direct/command all energy to work with you to achieve it. This way, you are honoring yourself, and by honoring yourself, you are venerating the Creative Force. Remember, no one can choose a thought, feeling, or belief for you that you do not agree to accept. And that makes you, "the creator of you" on this plane. So, let's give energy all the help we can to play with us successfully.

This opens us to the world of infinite possibilities. We allow the old beliefs that are not really ours, the fears lurking in our subconscious minds, the limitations used to define ourselves, and the powerless definitions we have accepted, to fall away so we can finally claim our magnificence! We must be magnificent; we are made in the "image and likeness" of the greatest Creative Force in existence! Once claimed, the Universe then says, "I want to go THERE and play!" This agreement is how we choose to create ourselves in harmony with the Universe's frequencies that will then deliver our desires to us. Like my friend E.T., the Universe conspires to send you back to the "home" of You: to the love of you, its friendship with all creation, and the open heart that allows you to embrace and trust that all energy is supporting your good. Then the signal you shoot out into the energy of All That Is will "find" you and bring you to a place of power and partnership with The Creative Force.

This signals the energy to no longer focus on fixing, redeeming, healing, and questioning, and it directs it toward the most powerful gift we have been given: Creation. The Universe knows how to create, but it is up to us to stop focusing on negative fixes and move into the harmony of love and joy where all creation happens.

You see, we ARE the place where it all happens, and it happens within us first. If you want more money, then love and be joyful about money. If you want better health, be joyful and love health. If you want a great partner, then love and feel joy around that partner. These are not just mantras; they are feelings and thoughts with a strong electrical charge that communicate with the Universe. I also want to add, that the more you ARE those attributes, the more the Universe responds to you. So, when you become the person you want to be with, it is easier to attract that energy in another person. The same applies to money and health and everything else! The challenge is to bring yourself to that state of being and "having" before the reality of "having" it becomes present! That makes no sense to our monkey minds: why should I feel love about money when I don't have enough? Why? Because that is precisely what will create it. When you go to a restaurant and order your dinner, you expect it to be delivered to you. You don't doubt it will come. You don't go back to the kitchen to question the chef or to check out all the ingredients he is using. You simply know and trust your meal will be delivered. You are the point where everything is first conceived and then created and delivered.

Now, that seems like a daunting responsibility. Actually, it is easy creation. It is just a choice—a choice to accept a new belief, a new concept. Allow yourself to know the world is round instead of flat so that you can expand your horizons. See yourself connecting with and being a part of the entire cosmos—all those galaxies. You are All-Energy, and all energy is you. You are working together with it, and the more consciously you work together in harmony with the Creative Force, the more vibrant and complete is your creation. This opens a dialogue between you and all energy, which accesses the Creative Force within this union to activate miraculous demonstrations.

The chief permission we must give ourselves to enter into this Universal dance of energy is: there is absolutely nothing we need to forgive. There is no need to redeem ourselves before we realize this communion with the Creative Force. In the eyes of energy, there is no sin. There is only "what is." We must start from ground zero, as in, "This is the first day of the rest of our lives." I want to invite you to look at your life as a great school where you have been studying. Sometimes you received a C, sometimes you earned an A, and sometimes you didn't even finish your report. Right now, at this moment, nobody cares, least of all the Universe. It just doesn't matter. Energy doesn't care about the past. But, if you keep focused on everything you think you've done wrong in your life, energy keeps following the direction of your thoughts and beliefs about yourself, which will not get you what you want!

So, let's give energy a fair chance to follow its best path! Let's make a clear choice to state what we want. Then, love it, feel good about it, and love ourselves enough to know we are worthy of creating and receiving our choice. Invite the energy of the Creative Force to partner with us in the creation of our desired results.

In the next chapter, we will delve into the specifics of making a clear choice. There is an art to choosing clearly, and it is imperative to understand it!

CHAPTER TWO: CHOICE

The individual, having free will, must consciously, with full determination, make the demand.

The I AM Discourses

Creation begins with choice. You cannot create without making a choice, because, as we know, energy must be directed. And we have to choose which direction to send it! You have to know what you want to choose, and then you have to choose it. Believe it or not, most people don't move past this first point, even though they think they are making a choice. We spend a lot of time thinking about what we want to do, attending courses about what interests us, and talking to others about our ideas. But that isn't really making a choice. It's merely thinking about making a choice. It's considering possibilities. It's taking time getting ready to see if we're ready! I couldn't take action toward becoming an actress until I made the choice to BE an actress. And yes, part of the action steps I took was attending classes.

However, without the clear choice of being an actress first, and following the breadcrumbs of creation the Universe dropped on my path to help me create my dream, I could have studied all my life and never worked as an actor! The clear choice states the goal you want to attain! It is the first major step that leads to your destination.

And remember, everything is energy, and again energy must be directed. That cannot happen until you make a determined choice about where you are directing your energy to arrive! Most of us are merely "hanging out." We are hanging out within our energy cocoon. But that never directs the energy where to go. And that leaves us floundering in the mire of "not knowing with no direction." We stay stuck in what we don't want to happen.

I teach seminars on self-creation all over the world. I have people whom I have never met, come on stage with me. Here is a typical exchange:

Dee: Hi, what would you like to work on today?

Guest: After a long pause . . . I guess, well, I don't have enough money.

Dee: Okay. Can you tell me specifically what you would like to address?

Guest: Well, I don't want to worry about money all the time.

Dee: Okay, so what exactly would you like an answer to?

Guest (getting impatient.) I want to know what I am doing wrong to create such a lack of money.

Dee: So, what do you want?

Guest: (Agitated) I DON'T WANT TO HAVE TO WORRY ABOUT MONEY

Dee: So again, what do you want?

Guest: (yelling) I WANT MORE MONEY!

Dee: Great. Now that you have clearly stated what you want, we can start creating it.

This stumbling about is how most of us think creation happens. We are trained to focus on the negatives, rid ourselves of what we don't want. To fix things. To dodge the responsibility of clear choice. And that indecision directs our minds and energy (and therefore the Universe) to focus on what we DON'T WANT.

When we were children, how many times did our parents ask us what we wanted? Not enough. We KNEW what we wanted: a toy, a piece of candy, going to the zoo, etc. And the answer to that "wanting," that choice, was usually a barrage of negatives about why we shouldn't ask for it; why we didn't need it; why we hadn't "earned" it; how they couldn't get it for us anyway. So, we became programmed to dialogue with ourselves in that very same way about want we want.

"I want to make a million dollars in the next two years. But I don't see how that can happen, because I'm not smart enough to build up what will create that, and I probably don't deserve it anyway." Those subconscious thoughts create a pattern of creation the Universe cannot answer. We literally dialogue ourselves from ever really making a clear choice about what we want! This ploy is actually making a choice not to choose. We are repeating the programmed answers to what we want that were consistently given to us as children. But those are THEIR answers, not our choices. Until we are conscious of what we want to choose, we just keep echoing the tapes running in our minds. Read the quote at the top of the chapter again. That is not how most of us are making our choices. Remember, the original meaning of "ask" in the Bible is "demand." Not supplication or pleading our case, but to demand, and to demand you must know what you are demanding. You must make a choice.

Now, making a choice is easier than you think when you don't actually think about it. If you want clear guidance, go to your heart. Your heart will always reveal the higher truth of any desire. Then, you can take that truth and direct your mind to focus on that! When we first go to our minds to find what we want, we automatically invite the subconscious monkey chatter of our past patterning to choose for us. And that stops us before we ever make a heartfelt choice. While we are repeating the arguments of our parents, societies, and religions about

34

impossible dreams, the Universe never hears our choice and demand, because we really have not clearly made one. We have limited our dreams, hopes, and aspirations before we even started. We never allow ourselves to delve into and utilize our imagination, where all things are created. Remember Einstein's famous comment, "The true sign of intelligence is not knowledge, but imagination." Why? Because that is where we create the vision of what we want in all its glorious possibilities! When we enter our imagination, we live in a world where our dreams have already been created. We feel it. We experience it. And the Universe picks up those signals and starts playing with us.

Jim Carey often talks about how, as a young actor, he would drive up to The Hollywood Sign, sit there, and imagine being a famous actor in Hollywood. He faithfully, as in blind faith, visited that Mecca in his imagination every night. "I would dream of being famous, and all the auditions I would get. I felt the excitement and the passion." There is an excellent story about Einstein as a young boy. He came home with a letter from school. When his mother opened it, it said that her son wasn't smart enough and wouldn't be allowed to attend their school. The little boy asked his mother what the letter was about. She told him it said he was so smart that they couldn't teach him anything. So his mother said to him that he would learn his lessons and how to create at home. That is the kind of story you want to tell yourself. Release the limiting mind tapes and only listen to the ones you choose to empower you! Be open to all the magic within you!

Not being open to that place of unlimited possibilities stops our manifestation before we ever start, because we fall into the, "What's the use" paradigm. Or, the "I'm not supposed to be here, getting what I want," or "The world doesn't respect me," or "I won't be able to handle this if I get it anyway," or " I won't be safe or loved if I demand and get what I want" paradigms. Our early programming keeps us repeating the same pitfall mantras, but WE are the ones imposing them on ourselves now. We don't encounter those stumbling blocks when we first go to our hearts for clarity. I want to be clear that I am not referring to "feelings" here. Not only do we choose (or don't choose) from negative feelings of fear or unworthiness, but our feelings can arise from old patterned behavior. Your heart is a point of clarity. Your heart always knows what you want and doesn't bring in the mental baggage of doubt. You know where your heart center is. Place your hand on your heart and ask it, "What do I really want?" You'll be surprised how much clarity you will receive. The challenge is to stay in your heart consistently and not allow your mind to defer to old beliefs and patterns. You must direct your mind (through choice!) to match what your heart aligns with, but only after you access your truth. Then, use your mind consciously to create new, empowering beliefs and patterns.

Moving past those old beliefs and patterns is a choice! Probably the first choice you must make. That choice sounds something like, "I am choosing and giving myself permission to ask for, and receive, all the desires of my heart." Go ahead. Try it. You won't get hit by a lightning bolt. Put your big toe in the surf and test the waters. I want you to feeeeeeeeel the power of being in charge of yourself, of absolutely knowing you can choose, then act upon what you want, and receive it.

Maybe this will help. Make two columns on a piece of paper. Pick one subject to address. Example:

Column 1	**Column 2**
WHAT I DON'T WANT	WHAT I WANT
1) I don't want to worry about money.	I want to be confident about money.
2) I feel like I have no control over money.	I know I am in control of my own energy.
3) I hate and resent money.	I choose to love money so I create it.
4) I can't see me having enough.	I choose to imagine having lots of money.
5) I shouldn't have any more than I need.	I love me and allow myself. to receive all the money I want.
6) It isn't possible.	It's all possible.

Now, from column 2, rephrase it this way:

1) I Am confident about money.

2) I Am in control of my own energy.

3) I Am money and I love it!

4) I Am filled with money in my life.

5) I Am open to receiving all the gifts of the Universe.

6) I Am the place of all possibilities.

CHAPTER THREE: THE ELECTRICAL CONNECTION

We physically are little units of electrical energy, and we vibrate and project electromagnetic thought.

John Trudell

The new physics provides a modern version of ancient spirituality. In a Universe made out of energy, everything is entangled, everything is One.

Bruce Lipton

In this chapter, I want to bring science into the creation process. Once we understand that there are clear scientific principles that support what we are doing, it is much easier for us to embrace creation as a known formula with expected results. It permits us to move out of hope and into knowing. It confirms that the Universe is working with us and creating with us when we apply the formula.

We all know that the heart and the brain have electrical currents. Our hearts are tested with an electrocardiogram, a machine that registers the electrical rhythms of our hearts. Our brains are tested with electroencephalograms, which monitor and record the synapses' electrical firings within our brains. We are, basically, electrical beings.

Science has proven that thoughts and emotions have electrical charges. We have only to experience great love or violent anger to experience those electrical charges in action. When we "have" a thought (because thoughts are actually chosen if we are conscious), its electrical signal goes out to the Universe. That thought also stirs up an emotional reaction, which is sent out. Without getting too technical, the Universe is one big electromagnetic force that constantly and consistently looks to match and amplify the electrical signals we send out. Whether positive or negative, the Universe acts without judgment, and its electromagnetic force will find your signal, align with it, and send it back to you reinforced. So, if we send out a love signal, that frequency of love is matched and magnetized to a matching frequency in the field, and is sent back to us, creating the experience of more love in our lives. If you send out a signal of fear, the Universe receives that frequency, aligns with it, and returns it to you, creating the experience of more fear in your life.

There have been some simple experiments performed by the military that Gregg Braden uses to show the connection and communication of energy. Leukocytes (white blood cells), which defend the body against infection, were collected for its DNA component from donors and placed into chambers so their electrical changes could be measured. In this experiment, the donor was placed in one room and subjected to "emotional stimulation" consisting of video clips that generated different emotions in the donor. The donor's DNA was placed in another room in the same building. Both were closely monitored, and as the donor exhibited emotional peaks or valleys (measured by electrical responses), the leukocytes' DNA exhibited identical responses at the exact same time. There was no lag time, no transmission time. Their electrical peaks and valleys exactly matched those of the donor.

The military wanted to see how far they could separate the donor from his DNA and still register this effect. They stopped testing after they separated the DNA and the donor by 50 miles with the same results. There was no lag time, no transmission time. Mr. Braden concluded from these studies that living cells communicate through a previously unrecognized form of energy. This energy is not affected by time or distance. It is a nonlocal form of energy, an energy that already exists everywhere all the time. A similar "nonlocal" transmission between subatomic particles over a great distance, called Quantum Entanglement, has also been charted by nuclear physicists.

The HeartMath Institute did a second experiment. In this experiment, volunteers gave human placenta DNA (the most pristine form of DNA). It was placed in a container from which the researchers could measure changes in the DNA. Twenty-eight vials of DNA were given (one each) to 28 researchers. Each of them had been trained on how to generate and FEEL their feelings. They then created a range of strong emotional responses. It was discovered that the DNA in the vials changed its shape according to the feelings generated by the researchers!

When researchers felt gratitude, love, and appreciation, the DNA responded by relaxing, and its strands unwound. The length of the DNA actually became longer. When the researchers felt anger, fear, frustration, or stress, the DNA tightened up. It became shorter and switched off many of its DNA codes. If you have ever felt "shut down" by your negative emotions, now you know why! Your body just shuts down, too. But the DNA codes were switched back on when the researchers began feeling love, joy, gratitude, and appreciation. This experiment was later performed on HIV-positive patients. They discovered that feelings of love, gratitude, and appreciation created 300,000 times the resistance to the virus than from patients without those positive feelings.

These tests led researchers to deduce that there is a new, unrecognized form of energy that CONNECTS ALL CREATION. This energy appears to be a tightly woven web that saturates and connects all matter everywhere. Essentially, we can influence this web of creation through our VIBRATION, be it positive or negative. Those vibrations are generated by our thoughts and feelings.

We are speaking to, interacting with, and are partners with all energy in the creation process. The electrical signals we send out through thoughts and feelings not only change the chemistry of our bodies and the realities of our lives, but they also change the Universe as well! And this is how we create our reality by choosing it with our thoughts and feelings.

Remember, the prime law of the Universe is that we attract what we are focused on. Neale Donald Walsch sums it up as: Fear? Or Love?

The scientist Bruce Lipton explains it this way: Your mind interprets the world, and that interpretation is translated into chemistry by the brain. Your perception (expectations and beliefs) of how things work creates the chemistry that is complimentary to your perception.

In other words, your beliefs (perceptions, expectations) carry more power than outside forces. You create your "reality."

Want more proof? Lipton goes on to explain it this way: Every live cell is like a battery. It has a negative charge on the inside, and a positive charge on the outside. It is electrical. Each cell has 1.4 volts of electricity. There are approximately 50 trillion cells in a body, which equals 700 trillion volts of electrical power. The Chinese call this energy force, "Chi." When we die, the cell remains, but the SIGNAL shuts off. He then explains that all disease is caused by two things:1) bad DNA creating bad proteins, as in birth defects; or 2) from bad signals, which can come from trauma, environmental toxins, and THOUGHT. What generates wrong signals coming from thoughts are our perceptions, and they send out positive or negative signals that our cells respond to! Literally, our genes are controlled by our perceptions. Science has proof that 95% of cancers are caused by *epigenetics*, or our perceptions and outlooks, and not by our genes. So, if we believe and perceive that we probably will get cancer, or be poor, or become an alcoholic because "it runs in the family," that perception will create our reality because that is the internal and external signals we are believing.

Cells often form groups, or "communities," to bind together. Basically, if a cell is part of a community, it must respond to the "main voice," which is the mind. The mind has a thought, and the hearts responds with an emotional connection to that thought, which then creates the internal and external signals we send out. The mind's job is to perceive and interpret the signals, and then send the information to the cells to control that cell's behavior and genetics. This process is why the placebo effect, where participants are given a "sugar" pill but told it is a powerful drug, works to create a state of health and wellness. The participant accepts and agrees to the successful treatment. They BELIEVE in the truth of it. Science has concluded that one-third of all physical healing, including surgery, is due to the placebo effect of strong belief.

Now, imagine the power your beliefs and perceptions have in our interaction with the Universe! We are the cell that is communicating our thought signals to the body of the Universe. The Universe matches our perceptions and beliefs, and the experiences of health and wellness in every area of our lives are created if they are positive, or negative, all according to our signals.

This is why we keep hearing statements like, "Thoughts are things," and "You create your life," and "As you believe, it is delivered to you," and "I am the captain of my ship," and "God helps him who helps himself," and "It's up to you . . . it's all in your control." We keep hearing them because they represent one great truth: We are the ones that choose the thoughts and emotions that send out the electrical signals that create our bodies and our lives. We are the electrical charge within the electromagnetic whole: when we accept that we are self-creators and choose the thoughts, feelings, and perceptions that support our desires, we become the magnets that draw its fulfillment to us from the Universal Whole. Said simply, we are the ones that choose what to plug in, and where to plug it in, so we work in

45

harmony with the entire electrical system of our bodies and the body of the Universe to get the completion charge we desire. The Universe responds to us.

I cannot express how powerful this concept is in your creation process. It brings science into the formula, which is vital. So many people continue to get bogged down with old beliefs: "I'm not worthy," "If I work really hard, I can earn a right to get what I want," "If I'm supposed to have it, I will," "I probably don't have the power to create," or, even more limiting, "I shouldn't have the power to create." All these limiting messages keep us confined to a life where we don't take responsibility for our creations, which we have discussed in Chapter Two as the first vital step. If we are subconsciously, or consciously, still being run by these beliefs, we never make the choice to make a better choice. And that sends out the electrical signal to the Universe that screams, "I'm not in charge here!" And guess what frequency the Universe must then match . . . you are not in charge. You actually magnetize being stuck. We then think that the world is "just happening to us." It is. Because by not making a clear, powerful choice to attract the desired result, we make no choice at all and set up our reality to not get what we want. That reality is what we experience because that is the signal we have sent out: I don't know what I want. I'm not in charge of making that choice.

These limiting beliefs, which we have accepted as the truths in our lives, have become the signal. Absolutely ANY limiting belief will be the signal sent out unconsciously, but still sent out, for the Universe to match, because we have not consciously made a strong choice WHAT to send out. Let's say we have the limiting belief: "I shouldn't have more than I need." That was one of my most powerful beliefs when I was young. (I suggest you go back to your childhood, ages birth through 8 years, and track all the limiting beliefs you were taught or had modeled to you.) If I am not consciously choosing my signal of positive choice, the signal of, "I don't know what I want," allows the belief that "I shouldn't have more than I need," to be sent out as a signal for the Universe to match. Why? Because you have not overridden the belief that you are not in charge, so this becomes a ripe opportunity for the subconscious to bear fruit to all the hidden, limiting beliefs of your past. For me, the belief that, "I shouldn't have more than I need," had been in place and activated since childhood! And so, for years, I always had "just enough." But that is not what I wanted! I wanted more than enough. So, I had to be clear, define clearly what I wanted, and choose to think it, feel it, and live it so I could override the original limitation and the Universe could match my demand for more! Then I could experience it in the reality of my life.

We must push through the shouldn'ts and couldn'ts and wouldn'ts and . . . JUST SAY EXACTLY WHAT WE WANT.

Because otherwise, we will never "walk out the door" into the healthy choice of our manifestation. When we agree to accept that, "I am the power that chooses choice, joy, and love," we begin an amazing dance with the Universe, where we allow ourselves to play the ultimate match game: "This is the life I am creating." Then, our perception of the Universe changes to one where we know we are taken care of and provided for in partnership with a friendly Universe. Here is an excellent example from a client:

This work has changed my life many times over the years I've been using it. Most recently, I felt like I had hit a wall. I was watching a friend of mine succeed when her videos went viral online. That would then translate into massive sales. When I was asked, 'Well, why don't you just use that formula and do that too?' I had every excuse in the book ready to go. It's not that simple; you can't control the algorithm; I don't have that type of content to use; no one will even see it on that big of a scale.

After being upset and frustrated about it for over a week, I finally decided to sit down and do the work. I focused on what I wanted—and the feeling I would have when it was happening. Then I got quiet and sent it out into the universe. I posted my video and watched as it only accumulated a few views but was diligent on keeping my thoughts and heart in the right frequency. I then consciously sent love to my friend, who had succeeded and I had been jealous of. I did this until I went to sleep that night.

Eight hours later, I woke up to the video having thousands of comments and over 1.5 million views. None of my other videos had ever been seen past two thousand views. There was no rhyme or reason; there was no secret algorithm code—it was just because of me. I chose to create it. I chose to feel it. I chose to manifest it into my reality. I chose to be in partnership with the Universe and align with what I wanted. GBS

This story perfectly exemplifies how an outcome can change instantly when you become clear about what you want, and feel love and joy about it (more about that in Chapter 4), and perceive a world where this is possible because the Universe is working with you! That is called, "being in alignment," with what you want. You know what alignment is: a position of agreement or alliance, or harmonic resonance. When you master these creation steps, you are in alignment. And the first step in alignment is knowing you have the power to create whatever you want!

That brings together the "Integration of the Whole Brain" into our creative process. Again, research has discovered that the heart and the brain are interconnected and working together. The brain has a "heart center," and the heart has a "brain center." When they work together in harmony, then we achieve the Integration of the Whole Brain. The HeartMath Institute summarizes:

Researchers with the HeartMath Institute and other entities have shown that the human heart, in addition to its other functions, actually possesses the equivalent of its own brain, what they call the heart brain, which interacts and communicates with the head brain.

This heart brain communicates with the brain via several pathways, and the brain, in turn, communicates with the heart. Between them, they continually exchange critical information that influences how the body functions.

Traditionally, scientists believed, it was the brain that sent information and issued commands to the body, including the heart, but we now know the reverse is true as well.

Research has shown that the heart communicates to the brain in four major ways: neurologically (through the transmission of nerve impulses), biochemically (via hormones and neurotransmitters), biophysically (through pressure waves) and energetically (through electromagnetic field interactions), HMI researchers explain in Science of the Heart, an overview of research conducted by the institute.

Communication along all these conduits significantly affects the brain's activity, Science of the Heart states. "Moreover, our research shows that messages the heart sends the brain can also affect performance.

One important way the heart can speak to and influence the brain is when the heart is coherent—experiencing stable, sine-wavelike patterns in its rhythms. When the heart is coherent, the body, including the brain, begins to experience many benefits, among them are greater mental clarity and ability, including better decision-making.

These changes come about because the heart, when it is coherent, sends out information that causes the changes via the processes mentioned above—neurologically, biochemically, biophysically, and energetically.

Although the heart and brain are automatically in constant communication, each of us also has [the] capacity to consciously and intentionally direct our hearts to communicate in beneficial ways with our bodies.

When we intentionally experience sincere positive emotions such as caring, compassion, or appreciation for someone or something, the heart processes these emotions and begins to become coherent and send out positive information throughout the entire body.

But most of us continue to believe that our heart and the brain are separate from each other and often work against each other. That is a false belief, but a prevalent one. We must go to our hearts to feel the highest truth of what we want, and then direct the mind to tell the brain to create the easiest form of its accomplishment. When we go to our minds first, our doubts and fears present themselves before we can "hear" clearly what our hearts really want from a place of love and knowing. When the heart and brain are working together, directed by our knowing heart, flow happens. We are aligned within ourselves and with the Universe. Then our signal is clear and strong. The Universe can magnetize it and deliver to us our dreams and desires.

Biochemist Moshe Szyf, in his superb TedTalk, discusses how genes are marked by experience. We are all born with social knowledge in our genes. However, how we are treated and taught to perceive the world affects our development more than our genetic predisposition. They have scientifically proven that if a child is raised with love and care, in a peaceful environment where they feel safe and happy, they are healthier and happier as their lives progress. There is far less evidence of autism, autoimmune disease, and metabolic diseases in such cases. He discusses how it is possible to deprogram genes that are not serving us, and program in beliefs and perceptions that "turn on" healthier gene predisposition. In other words, we can erase the memory of past experiences that automatically send us into reactionary creation. Like with a drug or alcohol addiction, we can unplug the emotional component that drives us to need the "fix." We can have control over what our genes express and set up a new genetic narrative. We create our lives with success, money, and relationships the same way: the happier, more loving, more grateful we feel, the more we magnetize the results we want. All this refers to the science of Epigenetics, referenced earlier, which is our body's way to change the destiny written in our DNA. And it extends out to all creation.

So, let us expand on this even further. If we know we are in communication and creating with the Universe, AND we know we direct energy, why not claim, "I Am the power that makes the choice of love and joy for all energy in all dimensions?" The Universe also has a heart and a brain! Its heart is vibrational frequencies; its brain is the signal from those frequencies. We are a microcosm of the Universe! A fractal of the whole. Imagine the state of love and consistent peace we all could live in if the entire Universe was balanced and aligned in heart and brain! That was its natural state before we showed up. However, the Universe is in constant play with US. It is listening to US. It is matching our signals! And if those signals are fear, worry, shame, jealousy, and greed, how can the heart of the Universe know it is love and joy? And how can it direct its brain to create that? We must accept that, "I am the creator of all creation," because all creation is in an intimate dance with the signals we are electrically sending out!

Therefore, creation begins with us. Each one of us. In every moment. That is what Gandhi's statement, "Be the change you want to see in the world," means. It is your BEINGNESS that is central to all creation. As the scientific tests proved earlier, all energy is inter-reacting with all energy. All the time. And it is our responsibility to consciously choose to BE the world we want to live in. Then, when we all do that, all our brains and hearts will be integrated and working together. The Universe is balancing itself in harmony with us. You must look no further than global warming to see how the Universe and nature are responding to humankind. We must make the choice of love, peace, joy, and integrity within our hearts, and consciously direct our minds to instruct our brains to create that choice to allow the Universe to work its magic.

That is when we truly come alive in the love and joy of being . . . love and joy. That is when the world breaks out into, "Happy Days Are Here Again!" War and struggle are over. Flow happens. All energy is united in one beautiful consciousness of love creation. And that brings us to Chapter 4.

CHAPTER FOUR: WHAT'S LOVE GOT TO DO WITH IT?

If I have the gift of prophecy and can fathom all mysteries and all knowledge, and if I have a faith that can move mountains, but have not love, I am nothing.

Corinthians 1:3

Love is the only reality and it is not a mere sentiment. It is the ultimate truth that lies at the heart of creation.

Rabindranath Tagore, Bengali Poet

Life is driven by love. The body in love is vital. The body in fear is threatened.

Bruce Lipton

As you can see from these quotes, religion, spirituality, and science are all in agreement: love is the driving force behind creation. This belief awakens and excites my heart, and is a knowing that I have come to embrace. When I purposefully stay in the state of love, my creation is easy and effortless. When I move out of love and into my mental construct of forcing and manipulating, creation becomes laborious and limited. This is my favorite chapter to write, because when I convince you of the power of love in manifestation, I know joyfully that your life will change exponentially.

I think the walls we have to accepting love as the most important state in creation are threefold: 1) we think it is too ethereal, something we cannot grasp, a poetic illusion and a state that we cannot actually direct, 2) we believe we must have a reason to love: they love me, and I can feel their love, and I should love them in return, or I achieved what I set out to attain so now I can love myself. I am "fitting my formula of success," so I deserve love, and 3) I haven't attained enlightenment, so I don't deserve to be loved.

None of these beliefs are true, but they are taught to us by religion, society, and family. They are our most limiting beliefs because they keep us from knowing the highest truth, which creates and supports all others: I Am Love. We are consistently trying to GET love and to EARN love, instead of being the frequency of love itself, which signals the Universe that whatever we desire already matches up with this mighty creative force. Remember, our thoughts and feelings are electrical signals that speak to the Universe and attract a matching vibration. So, if we ARE the frequency of love, and our thoughts and feelings are consistently broadcasting the frequency of love, we get more love returned: love appears as money, in relationships, in health, and in success. Again, that is why it is so important to CHOOSE them! As Christ stated, *"And now these remain, faith, hope, and love. But the greatest of these is love."* He also gave a pertinent instruction regarding love when he preached, *"Think only on these things."*

Christ was actually teaching the Quantum Theory of Science, which states that we create more of whatever we focus on. Love=More Love. Fear=More Fear. Or, to quote, *The New Paradigm in Science*, "This world is a giant quantum system where all things . . . are 'entangled,' intrinsically and instantly interconnected." And we know from chapters two and three that we must *choose* what we want, and then that is matched by the Universe and sent back to us as our reality. I often think of *Little Shop of Horrors* as a perfect analogy: if no one had kept feeding the plant from fear, it would have never grown big enough to devour them all!

The frequency of love opens all possibilities to us, as in *"with love, all things are possible."* And when we lovingly dive into all our possibilities with love, we are energized, excited, and passionate about creating them.

So, let's break down those walls! Yes, love is, to a degree, ethereal. You can't hold it, talk to it, take it for a walk, or produce a physical representation of it, etc. I often have clients saying, "I don't know how to love." When we break that belief down, it usually (the negative) means, "I don't know how to love me." I lead them through the process of finding their "love place." Your love place is easy to find. It is anything that, as soon as you think of it, opens your heart and puts a smile on your face. I use my beautiful dog, Freedom, or my favorite place in Hawaii, or my daughter when she was a baby. Again, it's easy. It's immediate. It's something that instantly takes you into the frequency of love, which you want to match to anything you choose to create. Then you want to connect that frequency to a strong command to the Universe, "Create this with me!" as you bask in the highest creative element on Earth: Love. Then you can daydream your dream goal while in this state. Everything lines up for you: the desire, the state of love that creates everything, the command to partner with the Universe, and the joy of receiving/having it. Remember, the Universe MUST answer your signal. It is the law.

The second wall is much more prevalent and ingrained: I need a reason to love and be loved. It's based on a deeper core belief we are taught: if I don't "earn" it, I don't deserve it. But love isn't money or goods or other services that we can "earn." The purpose of the choice of love isn't, "I'll give you some of mine if you give me some of yours. Wanna barter?" Most of us are taught this rule of exchange when we are very young. Mommy and daddy love us when we are good little girls and boys. We get better grades when we are good little girls and boys. God loves us more when we are good little girls and boys. So we learn that *what we do is more important than who we are.* We learn to "perform" in exchange for the love we want. To be "safe and loved, we have to earn it." But love is a state of Beingness. And what does that mean? Let me walk you through an experience of Beingness.

Draw a red dot on a piece of paper and tape it to the wall across from you. Now, go to your love place, and just send that red dot love. Love it like it is your most precious child or pet or your favorite place. Just love it. Now, allow yourself to receive love back from that red dot. Allow yourself to be moved by the connection of love you chose to create here. You see, a red dot does not give you a *reason* to love it. And you did nothing but allow yourself to receive love back from . . . a red dot! When you live in that frequency and complete the signal with the Universe, you are BEING love! Like the exercise above, we can simply choose to want to experience love . . . for ourselves—to choose to live in the frequency of love just because it feels good.

The greatest challenge we all face in this exploration of creation is Self-Love: the choice to love ourselves, whether anyone else does or not! But again, we are taught from an exceedingly early age that we should NOT love ourselves. We are taught that it is egotistical. We are taught that we will be judged for doing that. We are taught to give the toy that we want to someone else and participate in activities that we really don't want to do, and to keep our opinions to ourselves. These experiences don't shout, "Love yourself before anything else!" But in reality, who do we want to give everything to? The people we love. And we need to be at the top of the list to experience a state of receiving, right? Now, when we are in the state of pure love (and not egotistical love like narcissism,) the more we love ourselves, the more we receive abundance, and thus the more we have to share with others. Our "cup runneth over." But if we cannot love ourselves, we limit our creation and reception of our heart's desires, limiting what we can give back.

Most people do not understand that the principles of self-love, self-worth, and our value in the world are locked into our brain's mechanism by the age of eight years old. What is spoken to us and modeled to us in those first eight formative years are the beliefs we have about ourselves that we build a lifetime of action around. That becomes our state of being. They are the building blocks from which we create our lives. If you really want to find out why you keep hitting walls, look back and record what messages you received about yourself, your place in the world, and how the world responds to you. I cannot express how important it is to love yourself. The following client story is about how she changed her life by beginning to love who she was.

"I came from a family that believed in struggle and hard work. If you worked hard, you deserved to reap the rewards.

Usually, it was in the 'just enough' column. As I progressed in my spiritual teachings, I started to realize that I was living a life of constant struggle. I was deep into a big financial hole. I kept experiencing constant starts and stops and lived in inconsistencies. Finally, after really looking into my childhood, I realized I was playing a game with myself. And it was a game I couldn't win. I knew what my adult self wanted, but my childhood teachings made my little child want to always pull me back, so I didn't break the 'rules' she had learned about the way life worked. I believed I wasn't worthy or deserving of being taken care of with love and joy and ease.

"I decided, after studying *Conscious Creation*, that I had to rewrite my story. I worked with my little girl to school her into the beliefs that supported what I wanted: a life of health and happiness, where I created more than enough easily and joyfully. I did a lot of inner work on really loving myself, and it was so much easier than I thought once I made the choice to embrace it! I am writing this during the pandemic. There was a time I would have gladly dove into the victim scenario, accepting there was nothing I could do during this time, that it was my fate to struggle and suffer. I am overjoyed to report that with my self-love practice and my new self-definitions, I am financially secure while living in a safe, peaceful home. My job is considered essential. I worked through the entire lockdown and was in joy the entire time. I know this is because I learned to love myself. REALLY love myself. It is the signal I consciously choose to send out, and boy, does the Universe respond!" J.W.

You see, many of these belief patterns are genetic, meaning that they have been passed down to you from your ancestors, and you accepted that "that's the way it is." Like the beliefs, "High blood pressure runs in the family," or "You have to struggle to just get by," we can accept or reprogram what no longer serves us. I always tell my clients to be thankful for their parents and their upbringing, and accept the good things and write a new, more positive story about the negative ones. They showed you what you don't want. It's up to you to create what you do want now.

And now, let's look at this belief around the third wall: enlightenment, and how you need to reach that state to love yourself. Well, if you are run by the belief that you have to try to attain enlightenment, it means you will never live in the state of BEING . . . enlightenment. That's like saying, "I'm trying to walk out the door." You were born enlightened. It is your natural state. The pureness and innocence of a newborn baby is the state of enlightenment. Most children hold on to the connection with the Creative Force till around 4-5 years of age when they begin "being" schooled about their limitations or taught not to love who they are. Basically, Loving Yourself IS the state of enlightenment. There is nothing we need to teach or educate ourselves about enlightenment. We are born with that knowing. But we spend a lifetime of lost innocence trying to get back to what we knew when we first arrived: I Am Love.

When we allow ourselves to accept that pure, simple state, we "become as little children to enter the kingdom of heaven." (Matthew 18:3) Then we are one with the One, all is integrated, and we simply live in the state of love and create through that choice. Simplicity and flow are the natural rewards of enlightenment. So, there are no excuses regarding your worth to create and manifest. And if you choose to USE excuses and not love yourself, you and the Creative Force must abandon each other and your creation. Step forward in your power. It's safe. You will learn to expand with your self-acknowledgment. Remember, you can never experience BEING the Creative Force of you if you do not accept that you ARE the Creative Force. Because how we define ourselves gives direction to energy.

In the *I Am Discourses,* it becomes clear why the words "I Am" are so powerful, because anything you state after I Am is a strong direction to your energy and the Universe to create. Again, science talks about focus, and wherever you place your attention, that is where your energy is fed, and that is the signal you send out. So, however magnificent or limited you define yourself, your reality is created for you, by you. Ernest Holmes, the founder of *Science of Mind*, explains it this way: "If, then, we believe God is substance, God is food, God is shelter, God is happiness, God is life, and we wish to enjoy and experience that life which God is, we must claim for ourselves everything that we claim for God. For we and God are one. The mind by which we think is God." Ergo, we know, "God is Love," and thus we are also love. We must claim the frequency of Divine Love. Go ahead. Try stating this powerful truth: "I Am Divine Love." When we define ourselves as the highest form of love, which creates everything, we have our full creative power at work for us. Imagine how much the Universe will want to match that signal! Then we know and accept and use, "I Am the power that makes the choice of love and joy." Can you feel the excitement and power that opens within you just knowing you can create your life through choice and purpose? Can you feel your way into the freedom of that knowing, instead of thinking your creation is just happenstance and luck?

This is the awareness that changes your life: 1) everything is energy, 2) energy follows direction, 3) we direct energy through our thoughts, feelings, and perceptions, and energy responds 4) The more we love ourselves, the more power we have to create with because love is the most potent aspect of the creative force.

And that brings us to the fear of our own power. Our fear of being our own Creative Force. Most of us are afraid of being that powerful, again from our early teachings. The highest fear we hold around our own power is that we will be put to death for demonstrating it. That belief has been carried through our cells and DNA for eons. It extends way beyond the judgment of family and friends. It has its roots in ancient history, and in the age of old, fearful religious teachings. It never made sense to me that, "we are made in the image and likeness of . . ." and yet that same energy . . . which we are . . . would strike us down when we create as It does. You can see the oxymoron here. So, if we are One Energy as science, spirituality, and religion all state, that means WE are that energy turning against ourselves when we become too powerful! And what is that going to get us? A more limited, fearful life. It has to be, because that is the electrical signal we send out that the Universe must match: please give me what I want, but I'm scared *to death* to receive it! Again, is that a match to self-love? Not even close.

If we keep sending out that signal, we'll keep getting limited results and reinforce the belief, "No matter what I do, it's not going to work," leading to less self-love because we think we have failed. When we watch a little child trying to walk, we love and encourage them. We support them. Our love is unconditional whether they walk or not. Can we choose to love ourselves as unconditionally, so we can truly walk in our own power? Yes! But you must take that first step. As scientist Gregg Braden so beautifully summed it up: "Love yourself a little extra right now. You're learning, healing, growing, and discovering yourself all at once. It's about to get magical for you!"

The HeartMath Institute reinforces these truths: "The good news is we can positively change our individual and social field environments with attitudes of genuine love, appreciation, care and compassion, which moves us into coherence. *Coherence* is a highly efficient state in which all of the body's systems work together in harmony. Increasing personal coherence creates an alignment of mind, body, emotions, and spirit through the power of the heart. The field generated by the heart is called the electromagnetic field. It is the most powerful rhythmic energy field produced by the body as it becomes more organized during positive emotional-heart-coherent-states. So it's within all our power to create the field we desire."

Let us love ourselves enough to love ourselves unconditionally, so we can BE the state of love and affect our own creation and the hearts of others. Studies conducted in the HeartMath's laboratory have shown that the heart's electromagnetic field can be detected by other individuals and can produce measurable effects in a person several feet away. Want the world to be a more loving place? Start with loving yourself, and expand that outward. Then, truly, you are the change you want to see in the world. Then the world responds, and you know that you are, indeed, the power that chooses the love and joy that creates your reality.

CHAPTER FIVE: THE ZERO POINT

In the beginning, God created the heaven and the Earth. And the Earth was without form, and void.

Genesis 1:1-2

If you want a new outcome, you will have to break the habit of being yourself, and reinvent a new self.

Joe Dispenza, Scientist

Because there is such a law as gravity, the Universe can and will create itself from nothing. Spontaneous creation is the reason there is something rather than nothing: why the Universe exists, why we exist.

Discover Magazine

Let's begin by looking at the word "void." It means "nothing," "empty," "without form." If you are religious, you accept that God created the world from the "void" . . . nothing. If you are a scientist, you accept that the Big Bang, the creation of matter from nothing, happened from a state of extremely high density and high temperatures in the state of "no thing." So, basically, the greatest creation of all time happened from . . . nothing.

For me, my most incredible creation was my daughter. All the specialists told me I would never get pregnant. I decided God and I had a different plan. I lived for years imagining just holding that baby. And then the miracle happened, and I gave birth to this wonderful baby girl. A baby is a perfect example of BEING the Zero Point. It is an empty vessel, with all its possibilities ahead of it. It can imagine itself into any life it wants—unless, as most of us experienced, it is taught it can't create that.

The Weizmann Institute of Science in Rehovot, Israel, in a 1998 study entitled "Quantum Theory Demonstrated: Observation Affects Reality," concluded that we affect energy just by observing it. In other words, energy is just waiting for direction, a void state, representing the possibility of creating something from nothing. As scientist Gregg Braden summarizes, "It is a fact that the Universe is made of a shared matrix of energy (void) that underlies our physical world. It is a fact that belief is a language that 'speaks' to this matrix." It is better to create and direct the void from our desires than to keep trying to create what we want from what we don't want—old beliefs. Starting at the Zero Point is a much clearer communication to the energy.

The Zero Point is also the moment of absolute choice. Nothing exists yet until a clear choice is made. Then the possibilities open up for us.

The Zero Point is like the scales of justice. They remain in a balanced state of nothingness until given something to "weigh." Then they skew toward the right (justice) or left (injustice), depending on what is being weighed. Much like a thought, feeling, or a perspective, we, too, remain neutral until a question or desire must be "weighed."

That state of "nothing" is where the best creation in our lives happens. Einstein said, "No problem can be solved from the same level of consciousness that creates it," or from our old beliefs. He also said that imagination is more important than logic. And yet, very few of us create from the Zero Point where nothing exists, and everything is possible. We are addicted to finding problems and focusing on replacing what we don't want. That focus is not operating from the Zero Point, the void of NO PAST STORIES, and it reaches into the world of all possibilities. As Jim Carrey puts it: "dream up a good life!" One of my colleagues asked me how Zero Point differs from meditation. I told him that the end state is similar, but the process is dissimilar since you can't use meditation to *get to the state of the Zero Point.* As long as we are "trying to get somewhere," we don't get there because we keep trying. We never "walk out the door." So, in such cases, we are essentially directing our energy to send out the signal, "I'm not there yet." Personally, I just stop the world and am instantaneously there. No trying. Maybe that's why, according to the book *Power Vs. Force*, there are only twelve people on Earth that calibrate as "enlightened."

I have many stories from clients representing the power of creation when directed from the Zero Point, and I'll start with a few to help you find that state in your own life.

"To expand my business, I had to do many upgrades, including buying a new computer, which I had no idea how to use. It was daunting to me. I kept hearing, 'This is so hard,' and 'You don't even know how to set the thing up.' All my technical challenges kept pouring in. I realized those thoughts were coming from age-old beliefs that I wasn't smart enough. It occurred to me that I was trying to create something from all the limiting beliefs that were holding me back. I had just learned about the zero point and decided to implement the teaching. I opened my heart and acknowledged that I was ready to imagine that I had always been smart enough. None of these limitations were real. I imagined myself as a big void, and that all possibilities were open to me. I told myself, 'I am the creation of my world from the void.' Then I went into total trust.

"I told the Universe what I wanted and began. My first call was to Xfinity, who set the new computer up to my Wi-Fi so I could work on both computers at the same time. Then, with three calls to Apple techs, they patiently guided me through the process step by step. A call to Microsoft downloaded my new Word program for Mac. Apple sent me a return label for my old Mac, which I packed up, and FedEx picked it up at my door to be sent for recycling. My new Mac is working great, and the support I needed came through so easily! Easy creation! But I had to start, as the song says, 'at the very beginning,' without my stories of the past that kept echoing my limitations. I gave up, went to zero point, and let my imagination create this scenario of ease and success. This conscious creation stuff really works! And I love it!" JMP

This story so beautifully describes how this Zero Point practice can be used in our day-to-day lives to create everything. Our biggest challenge is to accept and implement what we learned from Chapters One and Two: we are responsible for the direction of our own (and therefore all) energy in the creation of our lives. If we do not accept and embrace that, we will not use our power to direct ourselves to the Zero Point, use our imaginations, and then dive into all new possibilities. And, if we don't, that will continue the pattern of defining ourselves as "not good enough to create who I am," which leads to less choice about being involved in our own destiny. We must embrace the challenge to look away from reality, go into the Zero Point of the void, play in your imagination, and create the you that YOU CHOOSE.

We all just want to keep telling our stories. And as long as we tell our stories, we keep living the limitations of them. I watched my father create amazing ideas in his lifetime, and I watched all those ideas taken away or destroyed by the "bigger" people like his business partners. That was how I believed "the world worked." Then, I saw my older brother repeat the same pattern: devise unique creations that were helping and creating marvelous things for people, and then having them taken away or destroyed by "bigger, more powerful" people. He had witnessed the same "realities" watching my father, and had adopted the belief early on that, "That's the way the world works."

And then it happened to me in my acting career. Not until years later, when well into my healing work, did I follow the breadcrumbs and put the pieces together. If I was going to change my life, I had to go to the Zero Point, where none of those stories existed and continued to run me. I had to change me by creating new stories that were supporting beliefs of the world giving me what I wanted: respect and honor from all the Big Guys in the world, and to know they were on my side! So, I am purposefully sending love to all who "hurt me" and letting go of the story that they did. I am choosing to respect them because that is what I am desiring. I am loving myself for learning this valuable lesson in my soul's progression: I create me. If life isn't showing up the way I want it to, there is a story somewhere that needs to be released to create from the great void where all things are possible.

The Bible says it perfectly in Colossians 3: 9-10: "You have stripped off the old self with its practices and have clothed yourselves with the new self, which is being renewed in knowledge according to the image of its creator."

And remember, the creator created everything from the void. And the creator is all thought and all possibilities! I also love how Abraham-Hicks channels the message: "If you will simply imagine your life as you want it to be, all cooperative components will be summoned. And even more important, all components summoned will cooperate. It is the Law."

Another client's testimonial addresses this perfectly:

"I had lived and worked in New York successfully for over sixteen years. I knew I wanted to move to Los Angeles, but my story kept bringing me back to, 'I don't know how to create this! There are so many things to get into alignment. I don't have the know-how. I don't have a place to live; I don't have a job. It doesn't make sense!' But the longing was strong. I decided to take myself into the world of all possibilities, and I realized that I couldn't get there without going to the zero point first: No expectations of difficulty. No fears of the unknown. Just that glorious place where everything I wanted was mine, easily and joyfully. So, I committed to moving, open to help from the Universe."

"I gave notice at my job, and almost as soon as I said, 'Yes!' to my heart, things started to open up. I kept feeling love and excitement about the move and telling myself this experience was 'all new,' and I could create anything. The first all-new sign was visiting the convenience store at the train station, where I caught the train back to my apartment. As I was getting coffee, the clerk told me how much she was going to miss me. I explained I had a couple of months, but I couldn't figure out how to get the items in my storage unit to my home. A man getting his newspaper handed me his card. 'I have a friend that has a box car, and we'd be happy to help.' Yep, let's hear it for easy!

"Everything was that easy. People and answers just showed up for me. I had created a great condo in Los Angeles. My friend joined me for the drive. All my belongings were taken care of. The only thing I hadn't created was a job. Somewhere around Pennsylvania, I got a call to detour to Arizona about a job interview. It sounded like a dream job. 'Stay in the zero point and follow the breadcrumbs,' I kept chirping to myself. I went, had a great interview, and left for California. I got the call: I was offered the job. But I didn't take it. It didn't seem in alignment with what my heart wanted, so I stayed in trust and kept imagining. I accepted a job in an industry that I knew nothing about. Within eight days on that job, I was promoted to manager, which included a new home rent-free. When I got home that night, my landlord told me she had to sell my condo. Perfect timing. And this house that came with my position was, literally, in paradise—mountains behind me, and the ocean on the other side. I am in heaven. Taken care of all the way when I let my stories go! Yay, to the zero point!" T.M.

You see, there are no stories at the zero point, in the void. There are only possibilities. I like to think of them as possibilities of Divine Love!

One of the telling ways we tell our old stories is through self-definition. By that, I mean the way we have come to think of ourselves. And most of those definitions are limiting. I'll start with some of mine: "I am the child of an alcoholic. My family was poor. I was the one who had to take care of everyone. I am a person who was taught that God loves the humble and poor people more. I am a successful actress who has been damaged in the business."

Okay, that's just a few of my definitions that kept me from creating from the zero point. Let me break it down:

I am the child of an alcoholic. Meaning: "I am a victim. I lived in turmoil growing up. I accepted that fear and struggle were normal." Zero Point Freedom: "I imagine me as a victor and a joyous creator. All I create is easy for me, and love and allowing is my normal state!"

75

My family was poor. Meaning: "I am a person who never had enough. I started 'working' as a model at age four to help support the family. I never knew/know if there was/is enough." Zero Pont Freedom: "I am enough, and I always create more than enough!"

I was the one who had to take care of everyone. Meaning: "If I didn't take care of everyone, I thought my family would die. And then, so would I. I had to give up myself to take care of others." Zero Point Freedom: "I create me, and the Universe responds. I am always joyfully taken care of. I am safe and secure in this world!"

I am a person who was taught that God loves the humble and poor people more. Meaning: "If I stay small, I have a better chance at Heaven." Zero Point Freedom: "I know that God is all thought, all possibility. God responds to my signal, and so I declare, 'I Am Divine Love!'"

I am a successful actress who has been damaged in the business. Meaning: "I believe the business has damaged me, and continues to damage me." Zero Point Freedom: "I am a successful actress who creates honor and respect for others and myself in all my endeavors."

You see, how we define ourselves dictates many of the limitations that prevent us from going to the Zero Point. Because if we are defining ourselves as "less than" in any way, we will never trust ourselves to go to that void where everything exists. We won't trust ourselves to know what to create, or that we even CAN create.

I really realized this concept after the release of *E.T., The Extraterrestrial*. When the movie came out, I got catapulted into the spotlight. All kinds of people, agents, publicists, accountants, rushed forward to help me. I became important overnight. Well, all my self-definitions of who I was became severely threatened. I wasn't poor anymore; I wasn't the one who had to take care of everyone—everyone was actually taking care of me! I was not, in the definition of my family, "humble" anymore. So, who was I? Had all those life-long definitions I had owned been wrong? How could I give myself the permission I needed to create a new me? I pulled back into my "smallness," where I was safe. It took me over ten years to say, "Enough! This reality isn't what I want!" I dug deep into myself to understand why this had happened, and I let go of all those limiting definitions of safety and smallness. I attribute this experience to catapulting me into the energy work I do today. This is the biggest challenge we all have to face: giving ourselves permission to define ourselves in bigger, more creative, more expansive ways, knowing we are safe to BE that! Through choice. Through imagination. Through love. And the Zero Point is the easiest way to make it happen.

Now, at this point, your monkey mind will leap forward to question and bring you into doubt. For example: "That doesn't make any sense. I have cancer now. That's the reality. I have to get rid of cancer before I can define me as whole again." Well, no. It really works the other way. Everything is energy, and energy must have a direction. We create our reality based on our beliefs and how we direct energy. So, as the good book says, "As you believe, it is delivered to you." THE BELIEF COMES FIRST. And most of the beliefs and definitions (also beliefs) limit our possibilities. Remember, we must look away from the reality that appears to be real, and focus on only what we want, feeling love and joy around that. It is true that, if you have cancer, you can remember a Zero Point where it did not exist. So, you KNOW there is that state you can access. Go into your imagination and see and feel the joy of health and wellness. Dwell and create from there. Send that signal out! I AM PERFECT HEALTH.

Money is another great challenge. It doesn't make sense to our minds to go to the Zero Point and imagine having all the money we need when we have so little. But remember, we must create a new "me" first if we are going to experience a new reality. Can we be open to the possibility that all this might actually . . . work? Like children, can we move into blind faith (despite what reality is showing us) that this just might be our salvation? After all, we were told, "Be as a little child to enter the kingdom of heaven." Children live in their imaginations, always ask for what they want, and trust they will receive it until taught otherwise. Until they are taught they can't, that they don't have the power to manifest dreams. We can embrace our little child once again and ask them to imagine with us the desires of our hearts. We can tell the little us inside, "Yes, you can redefine yourself. Yes, you do have the power. Yes, it's safe! Yes, it's all fun and love and imagination! Come play with me! Let's play in a sandbox full of money! Let's see money raining down upon us while we squeal and dance for joy!" We want our little child and our adult self to come together in the knowing that they are safe to be this powerful because we use our power of creation through Divine Love, which cannot be used in any contrary way. Define yourself as safe to be the powerful creator that you naturally are. Live in the imagination of your greatest dreams. As Jim Carrey stated: "You can have what you don't want so take a chance on what you love!"

Remember, the signal you send out to the Universe is the signal you get returned as your life's reality. What better signals to send than those of our joyous imaginings for the life we want?

CHAPTER SIX: ALL POSSIBILITIES

Combine a clear intention with an uncompromising trust in possibility, then you'll step into the unknown, and that's when the supernatural starts to unfold.

Joe Dispenza

The wind blows where it wishes, and you hear its sound, but you do not know where it comes from or where it goes. So it is with everyone who is born of the Spirit.

John 16:33

. . . the moment one definitely commits oneself, then providence moves, too. All sorts of things occur to help one that would never otherwise have occurred. A whole stream of events issues from the decision, raising in one's favor all manner of unforeseen incidents and meetings and material assistance, which no person could have dreamed would come their way.

W. H. Murray

These quotes are absolutely true. I have experienced many "divine interventions" in my life that seemed to blow in like the wind, answering my desires in ways unimaginable to me at the time. When I was trying to restart my career, I created a vision of a television series. I had specific parameters built into my vision: shooting in town, a creative experience, challenging, fun, and working with creative, talented people. And I didn't want to go through the dog and pony show with the networks to book it. I held this vision for two to three months. I didn't push it out there, but I felt love and excitement around it. When I was teaching acting one day, I got a message from my manager. They wanted to "Talk with me about a TV series." "It's a comedy." What? I hadn't done comedy for years. And it has a lot of improvisation. What? I didn't do improv. But I still went in to meet the director/producer and fell in love with him. He explained we would be working with "scripted ideas" that we could then flesh out with our ideas to make a scene. I had never worked this way. We played around with some ideas, and to my great surprise, I was surprisingly good at improv! And I was . . . funny! We put some scenes on tape, and as I was getting ready to leave, he said, "Oh, by the way, we won't be going to the networks. Can't really audition improv. So, you'll just be hearing from us. And I am doing everything in my power to get you this job."

I walked out of the room and just stood in the hallway. What just happened? I got everything I wanted in my envisioned series, including not going to the networks, and it happened in a totally unpredictable, impossible-to-imagine way! Months later, I booked the show, and it ran for three seasons.

I had done this kind of envisioning earlier in my career as well. At that time, I made an image board and wrote out all the components I desired in booking a big feature film: major players, good co-stars, a great director, and a part I would love in a film that would positively affect people. I held that intention over the summer. One day, in late August, I got THE call. "Steven Spielberg is offering you the part of the mom in his next movie about an alien that comes to Earth. Its working title is, *A Boys Life*, and it starts in late September."

So, let me stop this story here. I want you to focus, for just a moment, on the word "offered." That translates into no audition, no call-backs, and no sweating-out the process. About a year earlier, I had auditioned for a part in Steven's film, *Used Cars,* which I didn't book. He had remembered me from my audition and offered me the role of Mary when it was time to shoot his "little movie," *E.T. The Extraterrestrial*. So, later on, the Universe, in all its magical glory, had figured out how to create this part for me in the wildest, most creative way—which I could never have imagined.

And that's the secret: our job is to get clear, make a choice, feel love and excitement around it, ask the Universe to help create our desired results, and then BE OPEN TO ALL THE AMAZING POSSIBILTIES THAT CAN HAPPEN! Because in all my wildest dreams, I had never imagined a scenario where the premiere director in Hollywood would just offer me a lead in one of the biggest blockbuster films of all time. I needed the Universe to find that possibility for me! And I just had to be open to receive it.

And so do you. And that is not possible if we keep "retelling our stories of limitations and lack of possibilities." So can you decide, right now, to be open to alllllllllll the opportunities out there that will bring you your dreams in alllllllllll its far-out, unbelievable, and unpredictable ways. Believe that you live in this vast Universe of all possibilities? Then, with all the alignment steps put in place from Chapters One through Five, magic can, and will, happen.

So, let's review the basics that allow the world of all possibilities to be delivered to our doorstep:

First of all, many believe that IF we create what we want, someone or something will take it away from us. This doubt plays out in scenarios like creating a chunk of money only to have a big bill come in and wipe it out; or, you fall in love with the "perfect person," only to find they are married or faced with a dramatic health crisis when your life is moving along effortlessly. If this "take it away" belief is in place, you will have forfeited ahead of time the possibility of any incredible creation. With this belief active (remember, "as you believe, it is delivered to you"), your experiences in your life will match that death sentence, which ingrains itself even further, as the pattern keeps playing out! Instead, we want to know and direct our energy to know that whatever we create happens *continuously and successfully* as we reap our heart's desires.

We also cannot attract new, expansive, and unlimited possibilities if we keep retelling these old stories. "I've never been good with money," or "Every time I find 'him' he leaves," or "I'm fine and then something always happens." None of those beliefs allow all our possibilities to manifest. This includes the definitions we bring from family histories, as in "It runs in the family" (so I am limited and doomed). These are self-definitions, *limiting beliefs*, that we have taken on since childhood. To be free of them, we must choose new, empowering, expansive beliefs that match what we want now. "I am ready, willing, and able to be open to all the marvelous and fabulous possibilities the Universe has for me!"

And, of course, we must trust. And again, trust is a decision that we can direct ourselves to embrace. As we have learned in earlier chapters, we have to state what we want FIRST and continue to hold a focus and love around it to give our creation the space to be delivered in physical form. We KNOW that in 3D reality, we must trust ourselves to BE the authority that creates miracles in our lives. Here is a powerful statement that addresses all of these points: "I am the power that gives me the power to create and accept all new possibilities. I trust in my power to create happiness in all areas of my life!" So put your fears and doubts aside and move into trust.

And lastly, it is not your job to figure out HOW something can possibly be created. Leave that to the magic of the Universe. Your job is to know what you want, commit to creating it, feel love around it, ask the Universe to create it with you . . . and then trust the magic! I am going to keep reiterating this point throughout this book until it becomes locked into your brain! The following stories are good examples of people being open to all possibilities.

"I had been trying to get on top of my financial life for years. I just did not see any way out. I realized I had been THINKING about changing my story around money but had taken no action to redirect my thoughts to create something new. So, I started commanding it, 'I am Health and Wellness and Money!' Now, I decided to begin this work right after COVID-19 hit, which made no rational sense to my mind. All my outside work had stopped. But whenever those doubts came in, I stopped and reminded myself that, 'I am open to all the magic and possibilities the Universe can create.' Then the thought hit me to apply for unemployment. Truly, that thought had never occurred to me while I was still in the 'how the hell could this ever happen' state. And I started receiving the checks right away!

"Then, the realization that I owed back taxes because I had not filed for years rose from my subconscious. Yes, I had buried it down pretty far! I remembered that if we want to make more money, we must love and respect money. Well, I certainly had not respected money and my obligations for filing taxes. I realized that I was in such fear that I would owe lots of money that I 'didn't have,' so I just kept putting off filing. To make this short, once I took responsibility and filed taxes for those years, I ended up getting money back on every return! Now, that was kind of miraculous to me. I simply never thought that was possible!

"Then, my landlord offered me a month of free rent to help him with screening applicants. My former employer emailed to say they had gotten their PP Employee loan, and I would be receiving eight weeks of my maximum pay! In the last four months, I have paid off all my credit cards, and my credit score has gone up 128 points, and I now have thousands in my savings account. A year ago, I would not have thought all of this was possible. Now, I know everything is possible! You just have to be open to the magic!" L.A.

I love stories about these principles and their connection with money because so many of us were taught that the creation of funds lies outside of us and that we have no real power to create it other than "working hard." Sometimes, the belief that you must "work hard" actually pushes it away, especially if you are also asking to create some balance and joy around money.

This next story is how standing in your knowing and allowing all possibilities can affect your everyday life.

"I was returning from a trip to South Africa with my family. They were staying in New York, and I was heading on to Los Angeles. But I had a ten-hour delay before my flight would leave. My family insisted that I come home with them to kill time, but I discovered another flight leaving at 11 a.m. 'Forget it,' they said. 'They're never going to change your ticket.' I smiled and replied, 'You never know! Anything is possible!'

"I walked over to the first counter and asked if I could change to an earlier flight. The ticket agent said, 'Of course,' but then saw I had booked with a third party agent and the rules were 'no changes.' Now, I could have accepted this limitation, but I held firm to what I wanted and just kept saying to myself, 'Anything is possible. Anything is possible.' I took my ticket and arrived at the departing gate for the earlier flight and waited an hour for it to open. I took a moment to again get clear about what I wanted and feel excited about that, and then I said, 'Okay, Universe. It's you and me. Let's create this!'

"I stepped up to the desk and told the attendant that I wanted to get on this earlier flight. She smiled. It would be no problem because there were lots of open seats. Then she looked at my ticket and saw the 'no changes' indicator. The attendant looked at me. I smiled. She looked back at the ticket and said in a low voice, 'Don't tell anyone I am doing this because we're not supposed to!' And she handed me my new boarding pass. I called and told my family that I would be leaving on the 11 o'clock flight. 'How did you pull that off?' my brother asked in disbelief. 'I'm telling you, Bro, the Universe and I are hooked up!'" G.C.

As Albert Einstein said, "Logic will get you from A to B. Imagination will take you everywhere!" And one of my favorite "all-possibilities," stories is about health.

"In 2008, I was struck down with a major heart attack. When I was on the operating table, getting a stent put in my heart, it stopped beating. Needless to say, I am here and thriving. But what I learned from the experience changed my life.

"I started out acting on Daytime soaps with a few guest star roles here and there. Then my agent retired. I decided to take some time off and be with my family. I loved getting more involved with my daughter's life and being with family. But something was missing. I felt unfulfilled and sad. I thought about returning to acting, but at my age, being welcomed back was impractical and probably impossible. The years passed, my wife's career was taking off, and my daughter graduated from college. And that was when I got the news that I had a 98% blockage in my right coronary artery.

"I called my friend, Dee Wallace, who was an actress and a channel. I asked her what created this block. She replied, 'It's called heart dis-ease because your heart is not at ease. It is not living its passion.' I knew as soon as she said it that she was right. We had discussions about age, limitations, and how you should let the world say yes, instead of saying no to your dreams! I began studying with her again and learning the power of creation and being open to all the possibilities. Today, I am a very successful actor, making lots of money and living my dream. I have a beautiful family and lead a really balanced, happy life. As Peter Pan says, 'Just believe, and you can fly!'" R.C.

It is essential to remember about the kind of signals we put out to the Universe because that is what is matched and returned to us as our reality. So, it makes sense that, "There are infinite possibilities and I am open to them all," which is a much stronger, positive signal than, "I know the world is limited, and I don't know how this could happen, but I sure would like it, anyway!" The Universe can only compliment YOUR belief system, so be aware of that and create the openness for miracles to be delivered to you!

Another belief we must get beyond is, "I can never be God." As stated in earlier chapters, you ARE the God of You who picks your thoughts, feelings, and perspectives. So, on this plane, you are your own creator. I want you clearly to understand that if you deny that, why would YOU then believe you have the power to attract all possibilities? We simply must acknowledge and embrace that we are the power that chooses and creates on this plane if we are to experience the reality of that potential.

It is also helpful to open the energy flow of your chakras as you navigate your power outlay. Moving into extraordinary creation can be frightening if you are shut down. And fear, itself, closes your chakras and that flow for protection, and it blocks your outgoing signals to the Universe. So if you are making statements of desires while you are in fear, disbelief, or limitation, the Universe will not receive the direction. Always begin from your happy place of love and joy. The Universe receives your feelings even more than your thoughts!

I also want to address that old belief, "No matter what I do, it isn't going to work." Talk about a naysayer! If I were the Universe, I'd be really confused by this signal! It bleeds off our joy around creation before we even get started! And it certainly closes down all possibilities. Remember, *you built your life around this belief from when you were very young, so it APPEARS to be true*—like the sky is blue and water is wet. But it doesn't have to be. You can, right now, at this moment, choose the new, empowering belief, "No matter what I do, everything works out!" Then, the Universe can really take care of it in the way you truly desire. It will shout, "Now I have permission to deliver because they are open to the magic." At this point, life starts showing up differently, and you begin to experience everyday miracles from being the God of You that belongs in partnership with the Creative Force!

And finally, hidden very deep in our subconscious, is the belief that, "With good comes bad. With gain comes loss. With every positive, there is a negative." Again, a huge limitation in the world of "all possibilities." How can the Universe match limitless joy with such loss and negativity? Now, there's a signal we don't want to be putting out! How about, "I joyously create my good consciously and consistently!" That's a strong, clear, concise direction! That is a signal for all possibilities! And to make it even more powerful, we direct it to all energy in all dimensions (remember, your energy is hanging out in many different time/space continuums).

We now have all the principles in place, and it is time to dive into the practical, everyday applications to utilize these expansive truths. Be excited. Be open. Be powerful. This work will change your life!

CHAPTER SEVEN: THE THREE PILLARS OF ALIGNMENT

The character of our life is based on how we perceive it.

Bruce Lipton

When you find yourself on a vicious cycle, for goodness sake, stop peddling!

Comedian Swami Beyondananda

Most of us have been on such a "vicious cycle" in some way for the majority of our lives: creating the same patterns and challenges over and over again. I have become aware of specific "alignments" that must be in place to stop this momentum. The first we must master is self-love. Without these course corrections, our full manifestations cannot take place with the desired outcome. So, let's break down the three pillars of this alignment for our complete understanding. Begin by knowing that this refers to the pillars that uphold your creation process. They are your support system for the completion of your desires.

SELF LOVE: HOW I SEE MYSELF

This is not only the first but the most crucial pillar because your foundation cannot support the manifestation process without it. We have spoken at length about self-love and how most of us have been taught that we shouldn't love ourselves—that this is egotistical, and God won't love us, and the world will judge us harshly. We are taught as children to give our toys away if someone else wants to play with them, even if WE want to play with them! We are taught to make ourselves smaller and keep ourselves "humble." We are taught not to acknowledge our powers, our strengths, and our talents. All of these injunctions lead to creating "lives of quiet desperation," as Thoreau put it, and challenge our self-love.

After all, most of the people we want to give everything to are people we love! So it stands to reason that we must respectfully be the first in that line, so our cup can "runneth over," and we have even more to share. Self-love does not elevate us above others but creates our fullness so there is more to share. It creates more health, more wealth, more positive relationships, and more peace in our lives. Self-love gives us the quiet power to know and trust that we are the God of Us, so we bravely claim what we want, knowing that the Universe will hear us and deliver. Ultimately, the more we love ourselves, the more love we can give to others, which then gets returned to us, and the process begins again. I call this "Recigive": receiving

94

and giving all happening at once, like a giant bear hug between people, where both people experience this exchange simultaneously.

Self-love is the precursor of self-acceptance, acknowledging the powerful creator we are. Otherwise, we "accept" that we are "less than." I am reminded of the song popular at my daughter's preschool and why I chose that school. The words went like this:

I love myself so much

That I can love you so much

That you can love you so much

That you can start loving me

This song says it all, doesn't it?

HOW I SEE THE WORLD

I cannot stress how vital this pillar is to our creation process. You can reach a state of self-love, but if you perceive the world as one where you cannot fulfill your dreams, the house of desires crumbles.

Here I really want you to STOP. Stop. Stop. And have you now write down how you see the world. The following list might be a helpful guide. Circle which do/don't apply:

I do/don't see a world that allows me to be successful.

I do/don't see a world that respects and honors me.

I do/don't see a world where I can make more than enough money.

I do/don't see a world of health and wellness.

I do/don't see a world where all things are possible for me.

I do/don't see a world where I am loved for being who I am.

I do/don't see a world where we are self-creators.

If you circled "don't" in any of the above iterations, you want to redirect those perspectives because negative assumptions can thwart your self-creation progress. You need to put in place positive perceptions of the world, so our self-love has the fertile ground to flower and create. I am going to share with you a very personal and somewhat staggering story about myself and a realization that turned my life around.

I'll start by reminding you about the child's brain and how the child sees himself/herself and their place in the world is locked into the brain by the age of eight. I witnessed many incidences and discussions about how my father and then my brother were disrespected and dishonored by their business partners. How they had "lost everything" to unscrupulous people. (For more insight, check out my Tedtalk story on YouTube)

Cut to me several years later when my career began falling apart. I had made it to the Big Time, but at that point I had no understanding of how my childhood brain was running me and my life. In many working situations, I felt disrespected and dishonored. I felt I wasn't being listened to on the movie set. I felt dismissed. I became angrier and angrier at this perceived treatment.

That is until I began walking my talk and doing what I teach. I definitely saw the world as one that disrespected me. Now, I know that the world mirrors back to us *what is within us.* Ergo the statement: As within, so without. I knew this principle to be true, so I started delving into the self-definitions creating this lack of respect from others. I began remembering all the sad and disruptive affronts that had happened to my dad: A partner in his discount store had forgotten to pay the insurance, and then the building burned to the ground; another partner stole the fishing invention that he had created. He kept getting fired from jobs for no good reasons, which led to his alcoholism and abuse. Then I began remembering what had happened to my brother. He had worked his way high up in a presidential governmental office, but he couldn't stomach all the lies and the rampant abuse and disrespect for women there. Then, he created an amazing new spiritual company, only to have it taken away by his partner. You can see the pattern. And it was now happening to me.

I also remembered the beliefs I heard regularly from childhood: rich people are bad, and we're the good poor people. You shouldn't have more than you need. People in power rape you, etc.

So, this was my inherited view of the outside world: it was not to be trusted. It will take your success and your accomplishments away from you. And . . . wait for it, the big one: You can't respect them because they might hurt you. I was gobsmacked. I literally sat there stunned by this realization: *I wasn't being respected because I was not respecting them!* And the signal you put out to the world is the signal you get back. As hard as it was to acknowledge this belief, I knew that redirecting it into love and respect for all people was my "get out of jail" card. All this time, I had wanted the world to free me from my cell when all I had to do was release my negative perception of "them" and free myself. It was also the restart of a very prosperous stage in my career.

So, do not read through this section lightly. Go within. Is that one of the ways you are seeing the world and not allowing yourself to be the person you want to be out there? I'm sure you have your own tattered history. But, all this requires a shift of perspective. And that's a choice. And that choice can mean your freedom.

HOW I SEE THE WORLD SEEING ME

I'm sure you see how these three pillars dovetail together and affect the influence coming from each of the others. This is the important third pillar:

J. Z. Knight, in her channeled book, *The White Book,* explains how energy travels and is received, even before your physical presence might arrive somewhere else. She writes: "Whatever thought of fulfillment you allow yourself to feel leaves your body through your electromagnetic field, and it goes into consciousness flow to draw to you whatever will produce the same feeling from the desire experienced in your body. The more completely and intensely that desire is felt within your body, the more complete will be its fulfillment. And the more you know with absolute certainty that your desire will be fulfilled, the quicker the manifestation, **for absolute knowingness is a high frequency thought that enhances the expectancy put forth through the auric field, thus amplifying your power to manifest your desires.**" So, your expectations, positive or fearful, have a huge influence on the outcome of any meeting you may be undertaking to advance your success. Since I am an actress, I'll use the audition process.

Now, the audition process in the acting world is comparable to a business interview. You are "auditioning" to be hired. You are showing your wares. You are saying, "Please hire me." When I read about these truths, it totally changed the way I took meetings and auditioned for parts.

Before, my mental scenarios would go something like: "I'm just going in to do my best. I never get hired by this casting office, but maybe this time will be the one. I really don't even think they like me. They never redirect me or give me positive feedback. I probably am a little too old for the part anyway. Or not sexy enough. I hope I remember my lines!" Okay. All the energy carried by those thoughts, which I would recite in my bathroom at home applying makeup, were already on the way to join the energy in the room where I would be auditioning. Those thoughts weren't prepping the casting directors to receive me the way I wanted to be received. I was projecting onto these people that they probably would *not see me as the right choice.* That was the signal they were receiving before I ever got into my car to drive there. This was also the signal the Universe was also getting to match. Remember, energy is one, big, complete bubble unto itself. Information travels freely within it. Just like a psychic can pick up information from your energy, others pick up your thoughts. We've all had the experience of thinking about someone, and then they call. Or getting guidance to follow through on something and then realizing, when we do, the information's accuracy.

I can tell you, once I learned about this process, I began to CHOOSE my thoughts about how I perceived people were seeing me. My ritual before an audition became more positive: "They can see I am the perfect choice for this role. Our energies complement each other. I know they have only heard positive remarks from coworkers we have in common. They respect my body of work and honor my talent." What a difference, right? And it didn't just affect them. I walked into those rooms more confident, more balanced, more in control, and with more joy. I wasn't fighting through the negatives of my former perceptions. I was commanding myself to see only the positives.

One of the most successful stories I've heard around this realignment was from a client having a really terrible time at his office.

"I dreaded going to work every day. My supervisor was a negative, mean woman. I witnessed many women in the office, breaking down into tears almost daily from her abuse. I also was having many limitations put on me, so I couldn't really perform the creative endeavors that were my forte. As I began learning the principles of creation, I looked at my beliefs and perceptions about myself that might attract this hardship to me. To my great amazement, I uncovered thoughts that invited me to project my father's abusive and dismissive attitudes onto my supervisor. I saw her as an authoritarian. I saw her as someone who belittles others. But mostly, I saw her as someone who didn't respect me. Someone who saw me as a pawn to get what she wanted, just as my father did. I had no idea if shifting my attitudes would turn her around, but I decided to shift these projections for my own sake. I got up every morning, and I consciously made an effort to see her as someone who respected me, valued my contributions, and I made sure I saw myself that way. Each day she became a tiny bit better and more civil, and within two months, she was transferred out of our office to the other side of the building. The woman that replaced her went out of her way to verbally appreciate, acknowledge, and honor her workers. I was given expanded creative duties, where I could really serve more. I often laugh when I hear someone say, 'God works in mysterious ways.' I just smile and think, 'Boy, do I have a story for you!'" M.P.

So, again, all three pillars must be in place to support each of them. If I see myself as a great actress, but I believe "they" don't like me and see me as a limited actress, my signal is compromising and so is my creation. If I see myself as a great actress but see a world that "doesn't get me," the same applies.

And a hundred different variations on the same subject weaken the outcome of all our endeavors.

Now, some underlying beliefs affect the pillars we have in place. One is the signal of self-worth, which is an offshoot of self-love. If we truly love ourselves, feeling unworthy is not a match. If we do not see ourselves as worthy, it stands to reason that we cannot perceive a world that would embrace our worthiness or have the ability to see others seeing us as worthy. I see myself as worthy; I see the world as one where I am and can be worthy, and I see all people seeing me as worthy. Then I can truly know and implement that I Am the power that chooses joy and love in all my creations. And this puts in place seeing others as worthy, and because seeing them as unworthy is not a match to our own self-love.

Until the three pillars are in place and strongly implemented, most of us continue to live the core belief: "I have to give me up so I can take care of others, OR other people have to give up themselves to take care of me." We do not live in our power of creation if a part of our foundation is on shaky ground!

If these three pillars are not in place, we continue to live in doubt: can I do it? Am I good enough? Will they like me? Accept me? Will the world be kind to me? Is there even any room in the world for me? And so on. That energy isn't the energy of positive, powerful creation. It is the energy of limited, fearful creation. Since you are the God of You (remember?), which God do you want to define yourself as? It's a choice. Everything is a choice. And you can pick a new and revised choice at each moment.

Once we finally master loving ourselves, we want to expand that self-love into knowing others love us. And we want to choose to perceive a world where that "Recigive" love happens consistently: a natural give-and-take of love flowing from, and back to, the all-energy matrix! Then, it is possible to live in peacefulness and happiness because we Know. We don't live in a world of, "I don't know what's coming; am I safe, and can I handle it?" We live in a conscious and powerfully self-directed world of our own creation. We stand strong knowing that: I Am the power that chooses love and joy. And we know that love and joy are the emotional powers of creation!

When the three pillars are balanced and aligned, all possibilities are open to us because we TRUST. We trust ourselves, the world, others, and ultimately, the Universe. We know that all energy is on our side and working with us and that the signal we sent out is a powerful message to the Universe to partner with us in the creation of our heart's desires!

THE CLAIM

I see myself as powerful in this world. I see the world as a powerful place of Divine Love. I see all people seeing me and receiving me as the powerful entity of Divine Love that I AM. And so it is!

CHAPTER EIGHT: HOW TO CREATE

You had the power all along, Dorothy!

Glenda: The Wizard of Oz

The Universal Mind is not concerned with what you do not want. It wants to Know what you do want. It acts upon that.

Robert Bitzer

I want to leave you with a complete summary and a clear formula to use in your creation process. And it all begins with you accepting this truth: Creation is easy. Until you fully embrace that directive, you will hold on to the myriad of beliefs that underlie the erroneous umbrella belief: I must struggle to create. So, right now, claim with me (which means you are directing all energy to know and live it) that "Creation is easy!"

Great! Now, let us summarize the chapters as they present the steps of creation in order. In **Chapter One**, we learned that everything is energy and that energy must be consciously directed to manifest our desires. We direct energy with our thoughts, feelings, and perspectives, and in **Chapter Two** we learned to CHOOSE the thoughts, feelings, and perspectives that waft through our consciousness. We no longer allow thoughts, feelings, and perspectives of doubt, fear, and limitation to "automatically" fill up our energy reservoir. All creation starts with a choice, and the first choices pertain to our self-direction through our thoughts, feelings, and perspectives. That means that whenever we "automatically" default to victim thinking, we CHOOSE to reprogram ourselves with the positive, more powerful choices that will give us what we want.

The next powerful choice is becoming crystal clear about what you want, to CHOOSE what you want to create clearly. Most of us falter here because we were taught to think about what we don't want, instead of clearly and powerfully claiming (directing) to create only the positive results of what we have chosen. Read Robert Bitzer's quote at the top of the chapter. It says it all.

In **Chapter Three**, we learned about how we electrically "speak" to The Universe. Our thoughts, feelings, and perspectives have an electrical charge that shoots out into the Universe. Its job is to match that signal: not judge it, refine it, or question it. Match it. Again, that is why it is important to CHOOSE happy, powerful, and loving thoughts about what you choose to create, so that The Universe can match them with powerful results! If we are sending out "mixed signals," we get mixed results. For example, if you say, "I am creating more than enough money," along with, "I never have enough money," you are sending a mixed signal that limits the Universe in its ability to manifest the first directive fully. So, be clear and focused on the positive results you are creating, feeling love and joy around its completion and for you receiving it. To create this manifestation, you must release all of your old limiting, victimized definitions and stories. Remember, do not focus on "reality." That is what you've been creating from limiting beliefs that go back to your past lives, conceptions, and training from age 1-8. You are CHOOSING to create a new reality now.

We learned in **Chapter Four**, the importance and power that Love has in the creation process. Love is the most powerful creative force on Earth. We have come to think of it as a soft, gooey feeling positively associated with someone or something. But that reduces love to a reaction, not a creative force. We must choose to love what we are creating BEFORE we have it because it is the love of it that is the creative force that brings our desires into being! Many of us attempt to create money, relationships, success, and health because we don't have them. And we don't like not having them. So instead of focusing only on what we want, we "try" to fix that lack. It's like "trying" not to create what we do not want . . . again. None of that is about choosing ONLY what we want! Love all those things you "want," as if you already have them. Allow yourself to feel the excitement and freedom of already being in their presence. Let the Universe match that!

In **Chapter Five**, we delved into The Zero Point and the importance of going to that place where all creation begins. Again, it is impossible to get to The Zero Point if we hold on to our past "stories and definitions" because that point of neutrality is where everything is envisioned and created in a whole new place and time. For example, it is the place of health and wellness before your cancer. Or that place where money is an exchange of energy open to all who will create and receive it. Or that brand-new place, never experienced before, where you create that Divine connection. The more we are open to this *brave new world,* the faster we clear the past and start at the very beginning to create what we want. Again, this builds on the first chapters so that the formula all works in harmony.

Once we have all these practices in conscious alignment with love and joy, we must accept that all possibilities are open to us, as elaborated in **Chapter Six**. To limit our imagination and the Universal creative force in any way restricts what we can bring into manifestation on our behalf. It is the equivalent of sending out the mixed signal, "I am creating more than enough money, but I don't see how it is possible to do that," or " I am creating a healthy body, even though I think it's impossible with Stage 4 cancer." Trust me (and yourself) when I tell you, absolutely nothing is impossible for the Universe's Great Energy to create and match your clear direction and choice with love and surrender. Your job is to believe. And how do you start? By directing your energy to believe! Choose that now. That is always the beginning point: I choose. I direct. I allow.

Of course, all of these steps culminate into **Chapter Seven:** How you see yourself/How you see the world/How you see the world seeing you. All of the perspectives from Chapters 1-7 must be incorporated for our creation energy to be integrated and working together. Remember, you can choose to see yourself as the "God of You" that consciously creates your life. But if you see a world that will not allow you to be the God of You, or judges you negatively for that Knowing, you limit the Universe from working with you to manifest your desires. You can see yourself in that light and see a world that allows you to be that, BUT if you see the world looking back at you and seeing "someone unable to create," that also limits your creative force. So, what you choose to create must be in harmony with all three of these: I Am the God of Me, in a world that allows me to be the God of Me, and who clearly sees that I Am the God of Me.

CLAIMS

Now I want to discuss and clarify "claims." Whenever you are directing energy positively, you are making a claim. Staking a claim, if you will. Remember, the Good Book states: "*Ask, and it shall be given to you.*" The original Hebrew meaning of ask is "claim, or demand."

So, when we are claiming, "I Am money," we are demanding that we receive that from the Universe. When we command, we do not doubt. We commit. The first step again is choosing what you want, so you can clearly "stake your claim" and send out the command to the Universe to create this desire with you! If you don't embrace that power of commanding God, please know that 1) You were given permission to exercise your free will through choice, 2) All Energy is waiting for your direction (choice and claim) BEFORE it can intercede and partner with you, and 3) This is part of creating the miracles we were directed to create from the beginning. Choose to recreate the belief, "When I Am multidimensional, I am sick" to "When I Am multidimensional, I Am health and wellness through Divine Love."

When we stake our claims powerfully, through Divine Love, it sends out a strong, defined signal to the Universe, which it can then match and send back as the reality of our lives. So, it is incredibly important not to balk at and pull away from our power to claim: *This is delivered to me now!* If we do not powerfully stand up to our right to do that, we open the door to vacillation and doubt . . . neither of which is the strong direction the Universe waits to hear, and both of which limits our strong outgoing signal. So, stand firm in your convictions, your right to choose, and your duty to claim and demand. That is how energy responds. Without this knowing and this power, our Conscious Creating becomes minimized. This awareness of what you want, the commitment to demand it, and the powerful direction to create it are all integral parts of Conscious Creation . . . creating everything consciously and with a strong purpose.

GENETICS AND KARMA

I now want to clarify genetics and karma, as they have become "excuses" for many of us to not show up in our own creation. According to my channel, genetics are "beliefs that run through families that we have decided to believe, also." In other words, like everything else, the belief comes first. So, if we accept that "high blood pressure runs in the family," it becomes a belief that we then create and bring into our reality. Remember from Chapter Three that science has proven that around 93% of what we BELIEVED was genetic factors is epigenetic: our reactions to our histories and stories and our lack of conscious creation. All of that can be redirected. Even our genetic predispositions are physical forms of energy, expressing itself through belief patterns. Again, it can be redirected.

As my channel explains it, Karma is *the lack of conscious creation by believing we are destined to be without any power to recreate* [conditions]. As an example, "I am destined to live a poor life to pay for my extravagant past lives." That negates

ALL the principles of self-creation we have discussed. Believing in karma creates karma. So, continuing to hold the above-cited belief will create a life of continual poverty. Once you know you have the power and decide to create your own life through the direction of energy and choice, you no longer need to suffer and experience the effects of your limiting beliefs. Belief in karma keeps sending out the signal, "I have no control over my creation, and therefore, I am a victim." Conscious creation sends the signal, "I Am a powerful creator and I Am creating a new, expanded reality!"

I AM

The core of this entire work originated in the I Am Principle. God said, "I Am that I Am." In other words, God had to claim to be God in order to BE God. He had to define himself as God, the creator, so that he could BE God, the creator. The I Am IS your creative force. Anything that you claim after stating "I Am" is a clear direction to your energy to BE that. So, "I Am tired" pronounces your intention to experience "tired." "I never have enough money" is just another way of saying, "I Am a person without money," a direction to create more lack of money. "No matter what I do, it doesn't work," is another way of expressing, "I Am a person who can't create." All of these, and a thousand more "unconscious" statements, direct our lack of creation, not our powerful manifestations. In one way or another, most of us are declaring through the power of our I Am Creative Force, "I

114

Am a person who is limited." The highest claim you can make is, "I Am God," so you have the power to direct the desires of your heart powerfully. There is no limitation to the power of your I Am Presence, the Creative Force of the Universe. And remember, we are made "in the image and likeness of God." Ergo, we are the Creative Force.

BUT, if we limit ourselves and our power to create, we use that Creative Force to manifest . . . lack. Limitation. Fear. Doubt. So yes, we can use the greatest creative force on Earth to expand or contract. It is up to us to use it wisely, to truly learn the power of our free will. When we direct from the power of our I Am Presence, we send out the signal, "I Am the God of me, choosing_____." Make sure that what fills that blank space reflects our Power through Divine Love, peace, balance, joy, harmony, health, wellness, and wealth everywhere in our lives. Remember, the Universe does not judge: its job is to match your direction. Then you truly know and experience that, "I Am the Power that chooses joy and love in the creation of my life, and my heart is open!"

FOCUSED CLAIMS

One thing I want to encourage is keeping the direction of your life and your wishes SIMPLE. Remember, it's easy. Make a choice, commit to it, feel love and joy around it, ask (direct) the Universe to partner with you in creating it, be open to all possibilities, and allow yourself to receive!

What most often challenges my clients is they stress over saying the right words. Below I'm going to offer some strong claims on several subjects to get the idea:

MONEY

I Am creating more than enough right now, and consistently.

I Am worthy to receive all the money I desire, and my consciousness does amazing, loving things with it!

I trust that I Am the power that creates money in my life. It all starts within me!

I direct money to create peace, harmony, love, and abundance in my life through Divine Love. Money is my good friend who cares for me.

I easily and successfully handle all the money I attract.

I Am open to all the fabulous ways money can come to me. I Am open to all possibilities!

HEALTH AND WELLNESS (All subjects)

I Am the creation of health and wellness through self-love.

The more I love myself, the healthier I Am!

All energy is integrated completely from all dimensions into my Divine Self.

I know that the more I come forward for myself, the more I Am rewarded by the Universe, and the healthier my life is!

I Am energy, and I direct my energy to create health and wellness everywhere in my life!

The more I value myself, the more I support myself with love and health and wellness in my life!

RELATIONSHIPS

I see all people, and all energy in the world, as supporting me in love and honor.

I can handle all my good because I created it.

I attract the perfect relationships where I can come forward for myself in every way!

I choose to be the God of Me who creates relationships of love, respect, honor, communication, and joy, and I Am attracting those to me now and consistently.

I respect all energy, and all energy respects me.

All positive relationships have time for me.

LIFE CREATION

I Am the God of Me who creates my life purposefully.

I know what I want, and I choose it and commit to the creation of it.

No matter what I do, it works!

I was born good enough, and I accept my magnificence.

I Am that I Am (YOU are the creative force that defines you).

I always come through for me, so God and the Universe can always come through for me.

Remember, the above are not statements; they are strong directions/commands to all energy to create Itself in those terms. The more you accept the power of your own creation and live it consciously and consistently, the more your life shows up in miraculous ways. Like this:

As you know, I am an actress. At the beginning of March 2020, the coronavirus took over the world. All the studios shut down, and the first thought I had was, "How will I make a living and survive this year when I can't work?" But I caught myself really quickly and turned that thought around to what I know is the truth: *I am the creation of money in my life. I will ask every day, "What can I create today?" I direct all of me and the Universe to create consistent money flow through joy and Divine Love.*

I would begin each day with the question, "What can I create today? I am open to money from anywhere and all possibilities!" And then I would listen. And follow. And create. And be open to all possibilities. The first month, I received a check for thousands that I didn't even know had been negotiated on my behalf. The second month, I was hired to do a project that I could shoot from home. In the third month, I decided to reach out to friends who were icons in the horror industry, and we created an amazing little short film called "Stay Home", which is doing amazingly well on YouTube! The next month I was offered a film, totally shot in a compound that was COVID safe, which paid me a decent salary. In the fifth month, I created a fantastic healing package that friends in the industry helped me promote into a huge success. I told the Universe that my first intention was to serve in the highest way, and I was willing to receive good pay for my service. In the end, everyone won. Big.

The next month I unexpectedly received two large residual checks in the mail from shows I didn't even know were running anymore! When October arrived, I had offers to do signings and zoom meetings with fans, which my appearance agent worked very hard to create. This energy catapulted us into November, where I had the beautiful opportunity to serve again, doing some astounding affiliate healing programs that garnered a lovely financial blessing. And then December came, my favorite time of the year. "It's okay," I told myself, "You have enough. All the studios close down for the holidays." Wow. You would think I'd have caught that limiting thought before it wafted out to the Universe. But the important thing is . . . I caught it. "Nope. I am open to and creating all possibilities. Then a TV audition came. Then the booking of one episode. This turned into two episodes, and now just turned into three episodes, a recurring part in a great show! Now, even January 2021 is starting off with a bang!

You see, I could have never foreseen these specific happenings. I didn't even know most of these opportunities were brewing out there. But then, that was not my job. My job was to affirm that the creation of money began WITHIN me, and feel joy and excitement about what was delivered from the Universe. My job was to hold myself in the knowing that all is well, I am taken care of, and I am worthy of all the good I call in. My job was to trust . . . myself and the Universe.

So be your own cheerleader, creator, knower, giver, receiver, and confidant. The Universe is the best partner you will ever have. Hire it today as your coworker and cocreator and get busy. There are miracles out there awaiting you . . . and they will show up every day as just the way life is!

EXERCISES

The following are some life-changing exercises to guide you through your exploration. If you do these consciously and consistently, you will find that you, and your life, become more powerful in meaningful ways.

UNCOVERING YOUR CORE BELIEFS

Begin by making a list of the different life subjects you are focused on: money, relationships, health, etc. Under each, write out what you were verbally taught about this subject. For example, were you told that it was okay to make all the money you desired, that everyone would love you, and that you had the power and the talent to create anything you wanted? If you are like most of us, probably not. Become aware of the limiting concepts taught to you in childhood. Then, look at what your parents modeled to you in their behavior. How did THEY deal with and handle money, and what were their belief systems about it? Their beliefs and behavior helped create how YOU look at the world, your place in it, and influenced your ability to create it.

If you find limiting, fearful, and judgmental beliefs (and you will), look to see if you "accepted" those beliefs as the "way the world is." Those beliefs are walls that keep you from really branching out into your most potent creations. Make a list of life subjects, i.e., money, relationships, health, and success. Write down under each, your stream-of-consciousness flow about them. Then to the right, add the positive belief that will give you what you want!

For example:

We are poor, and God loves poor people more.	I choose to define myself as wealthy, knowing the Universe accepts me and my joyful creation.
Rich people are selfish and don't share.	I choose to do wonderful giving things with my abundance of money.

KNOWING CLEARLY WHAT YOU WANT NOW

The easiest way to do this exercise is to return to your childhood. Remember, our brains are fixed around how we see ourselves and how we see the world by age eight. So, whatever beliefs you formed in your early, formative years, you have been creating your world with them ever since that time! Start by making three columns on a piece of paper.

What I Don't Want	What I Want	What I Am Creating Now
I don't want a lack of money.	I want an abundance of money.	I Am creating an abundance of money now!
I don't want to be sick.	I want to be healthy and feel great.	I Am creating health and wellness now! I feel great!
I don't want to be alone.	I want a significant other.	I Am creating a great partner who honors and respects me!

Then, get up each day and DIRECT your energy and the Universe's: Today, I Am _____ and list everything in the final column—that I Am creating now. Do this AFTER you connect with your love place. Remember, feelings speak the loudest. Match your desires with as much love, excitement, and joy as you can conjure.

THE BREATHING EXERCISE

This is the most powerful exercise the Channel has to offer. Science has now confirmed the importance of deep breathing in opening the Vagus nerve, which aids in energy flow and communication. Ask the Universe to partner with you in the creation of what you want, then:

1) Go to your love place (anything that opens your heart and puts a smile on your face). Dwell in that love and joy.

2) Take a deep breath, inhaling to the count of four.

3) Smile.

4) Exhale slowly, saying the positive statement that creates what you want, i.e., I Am money! Be sure you say this claim to yourself with great passion and joy.

Repeat this for ten minutes. The time will fly by! You can use this exercise with any subject you choose AS LONG AS IT IS STATED IN THE POSITIVE.

I do this exercise daily. Remember, what you create today shows up in your life in the days and months to follow.

THE ELATION EXERCISE

This can be a lot of fun! Picture a three-year-old who is so excited to get what he wants that his whole body shakes! He stamps his feet and wiggles his arms in anticipation. You will be that little child, jumping and wiggling your body in joy as you proclaim: I'm so happy I have lots of money! I'm so happy I have lots of money! I'm so happy I have lots of money!

Of course, you can also state: I'm so happy that I'm healthy! Or, I'm so happy I have a beautiful partner. Or, I'm so happy I'm so successful! The point is to tell your brain, "Look! I already am experiencing having this new reality, and it is so joyful and full of love! Whopeeeeeeeeeeeee!"

Remember, you are not "lying" to yourself. You are directing energy to create this reality while you are feeling the experience of already having it! That's how magic works.

ALL POSSIBILITIES

Close your eyes. Picture the Universe and its numberless galaxies that go on and on forever. See the beauty and the grandeur of our boundless Universe. This expanse is where all possibilities exist. Acknowledge that all your desires are alive out there rushing toward you with love and joy. Be at one with the Universe and just hang out with the vastness of what is possible. Direct all your heart's desires to come to you, knowing you are safe and secure in this world and can receive them.

THE LIGHT

This is a potent exercise. I especially love to use it to create health and wellness in my body and my brain.

Go to your love place in your heart. Let it expand into a brilliant bright light. Then direct that light to travel through your body and brain, filling it with "the light of love." Remember, love is the greatest power we can employ. It creates and heals everything! Keep expanding that light until it fills your entire body and brain. Be aware that this light is creating health throughout your body and brain, your whole being. Send it gratitude for its brilliance and love. Know YOU are creating an absolute state of health with it.

GLOSSARY OF TERMS

Affirmations: Strong positive statements of declaration. They differ from claims because they are not necessarily considered strong commands but more like "hopes and dreams."

All-Energy: Everything is energy. This term encompasses and represents All That Is.

Align: When we talk about "align with" or "being aligned," we mean to "line up with." You can also express this as "being in harmony with." There is no discord present. When we are aligned, we are fully one with what we are aligning with.

Beingness: When we ARE the frequency of the state we desire, we are in the state of Beingness, not wanting. We become the frequency of the thing we want. The easiest way to achieve this is through love.

Chakras: Centers of energy in your body that correspond with different body organs and energetic patterns. When your chakras are open, balanced, and spinning in the right direction, your energy flows through the open chakras more fluidly. It makes Creation easier and manifestation more complete. As with everything, use your power of choice and direction to keep your chakras open.

Channel: A Channel is a form of communication with energy and energetic information. It is accessed through intention. All information is available to anyone who asks, as in, "Ask, and you will receive." The biggest challenges in working with your channel are 1) self-trust and 2) understanding the information you receive.

Channeling: The art of bringing in information from the Universe through your channel.

Chi: In Chinese philosophy, it is the circulating life force energy inherent in all things. In traditional Chinese medicine, like acupuncture, the balance of positive and negative forces in the body essential for good health.

Coherence: The state of being naturally connected and in the flow with a greater whole.

Conscious Creation: The art of living and creating consciously through choice, focus, and direction.

Creative Force: A term representing the highest form of creation: God, Buddha, Krishna, etc., depending on your belief system. It is also the power with which you create, as you "use the God that you are" as your Creative Force.

Electromagnetic Force: One of the four fundamental forces in the universe. It describes how charged particles react to electric and magnetic fields, and the fundamental links between them. It is responsible for atomic structure and all chemical reactions.

Epigenetics: The study of how your behavior and environmental influences can cause changes that affect your genes.

Fractal: A geometric figure where each of its parts reflects the whole structure or are self-similar across different scales. It is useful in describing partly random or seemingly chaotic phenomena such as crystal growth, fluid turbulence, and galaxy formation. Energetically, we are a fractal of the Creative Force.

Harmonizing: When your energy is in accord or agreement with another field of energy.

I Am: This is the holy expression for the name of God and is the highest aspect of yourself. Whatever follows the statement "I Am" is a direction of energy and a declaration of self-definition for manifestation by your God Principle.

Love Place: The love place is anything that opens your heart and puts a smile on your face. A pet, a place in nature, a baby— whatever automatically takes you into love without attachment. This is where you want to go energetically to connect with your heart's desire. Begin all creation from this place.

Open Heart: Much like the chakras, our hearts need to be open for the energy of creation to flow through us. An open heart also helps you hear Truth more clearly, to stay in that place where you "know you know," and allows you access to your love place.

Nonlocal: An effect that transcends local time and space, or happens instantaneously, like remote healing.

Recigive: The art of receiving and giving as one complete act that happens at the same moment in time.

Resonate: When your frequency is aligned with another's or is the same frequency as Source.

Quantum Entanglement: In quantum physics, entangled particles remain connected so that actions performed on one affect the other, even when separated by great distances. It explains nonlocal events.

Quantum Theory: The theoretical basis of modern physics that explains the nature and behavior of matter and energy on the atomic and subatomic levels. Even though its description of systems starts at the microscopic scale, the effects can extend to phenomena at macroscopic levels like star clusters, or even in everyday life, like explaining why hot objects glow red or how fluorescent lights work.

Universe: The cosmos or creative force of all energy that responds to our direction.

Vibrations: A person's energetic state, the atmosphere of a place, or the associations of an object as communicated and felt by others and the Universe at large.

Whole Brain: The totality of the brain, including the brain's "heart."

Zero Point: The point of energy where all possibilities exist, and new direction manifests new creation. There is no "before" or history at the Zero Point.

BIBLIOGRAPHY

Braden, Gregg. *The Divine Matrix*. Los Angeles, CA: Hay House Inc., 2008

Braden, Gregg. *The Spontaneous Healing of Belief*. Los Angeles, CA: Hay House Inc., 2009

Church, Dawson. *Mind to Matter*. Los Angeles, CA: Hay House UK, 2019

Dispenza, Joe. *Breaking The Habit of Being Yourself*. Los Angeles, CA: Hay House Inc., 2013

Lipton, Bruce H. *The Biology of Belief*, Los Angeles, CA: Hay House, 2016

Walsch, Neale Donald. *The Complete Conversations with God*. New York, NY: TarcherPerigee, 2005.

ABOUT THE AUTHOR

Dee Wallace is an internationally known actress with over 200 film credits, including *E.T.* and *Cujo*. She is also a well-respected spiritual channel with clients throughout the United States, Canada, Europe, and Asia. She has authored seven books on the art of self-creation and has a call-in radio show that has aired over 500 episodes. Dee does daily personal sessions in her home and on the phone. She also creates monthly webinars on various important topics. Ms. Wallace has appeared on every major talk show, including *Oprah* and *Good Morning America*, and was a keynote guest speaker at events throughout America, Canada, Tokyo, China, Australia, New Zealand, and England. Her message of self-love, self-creation, and directing energy continues to grow worldwide.